Jel Walter

FULL TILT BOOGIE

A journey into autism, fatherhood,
and an epic test of man and beast

Abridged Edition
© *2016 By Hal Walter*

Out There Publishing
307 Centennial Drive
Westcliffe, Colorado 81252

www.hardscrabbletimes.com
jackassontherun@gmail.com

Cover Painting

Autumn Alchemy
by Shari Ubechel
www.earthandspirit.net

ISBN: 978-0-9677148-1-3

Library of Congress Control Number: 2014916747

"I wanted you to see what real courage is . . . It's when you know you're licked before you begin but you begin anyway and you see it through no matter what. You rarely win, but sometimes you do."

— **Harper Lee, *To Kill a Mockingbird***

In the fresh moonlight she floated on a loose rope like some strange creature out of a dream, part "racehorse," part moonbeam. Her long ears trailing shadows on the gravel, and her sleek form slipping softly through the night air. Not exactly of this world. A locomotive with a heart and 10 million years of selection, both natural and supernatural, she was everything the past had conspired to bring to this moment and in the balance of her very being, everything her future held.

CHAPTER 1

IN THE SUMMER OF 1986 Mary and I were engaged to be married. We'd been together as a couple on and off, but mostly on, since meeting in college as freshmen eight years before. The engagement was short and Mary's parents would not accept any marriage unless the ceremony was performed by a Catholic priest. I really had no problem with that — someone had to do it — except there was the matter of the church's required marriage classes which I refused to attend. After some gnashing of teeth by the family and discussion with the parish, and since the family was prominent in the church, it was decided that a couple of sit-down discussions with the priest would suffice.

We met with the priest in a small windowless room at the church. He told us of the meanings and challenges of marriage and then went through the process of explaining the ceremony, and the questions that would precede the vows, at last reaching the one question that truly mattered to the church.

"Will you accept children lovingly from God, and bring them up according to the law of Christ and his Church?"

He looked at me and then at Mary and then back at me. There was silence.

"No," I finally said. "I don't want to have children."

The priest looked down and chuckled, as if he'd heard this same line from so many young men before me. He sat back and clasped his hands before him. I wondered if the wedding actually might be off after all.

"Well," he said, "could you just say you would accept children lovingly from God *on this day*?"

My mind swirled as I thought deeply but quickly about the absurdity I believed organized religion to be, not to mention the irony of using literary license in dealings with God, who surely had the ability to get to the bottom of such matters. The double, maybe even triple, entendre played over and over in my head as I thought it over. "Would you accept children lovingly from God *on this day*?"

"Sure," I said. "OK."

≈

On the last Sunday of July, 2012, I was bounding over and around rocks and boulders, racing down Mosquito Pass in the 64th World Championship Pack-Burro Race.

My eyes, brain, and legs were quickly and carefully — and almost unconsciously — planning each step a split second before setting my feet, while simultaneously guiding my burro Laredo over this rugged terrain. We had made it to the summit of the 13,187-foot pass, neck and neck with George Zack and his burro Jack, and now with about 10 miles left in the 29-mile race it had come down to these two teams and the pace was picking up.

After rounding a sharp right switchback I drove Laredo ahead to take the lead, and suddenly I tripped on a rock and pitched forward toward the roadbed, flying, turning, tucking my head and landing on the back of my head and left shoulder. The rest of my body flowed and flipped with the momentum and landed with a whump — a complete somersault onto the rocky roadbed. I held tight to the lead rope and was dragged a short distance with my right elbow auguring into the road before finding the presence to spit out the word "whoa."

Laredo stopped in his tracks.

George stopped too. He asked if I was OK and handed me my sunglasses, which had flown during the fall. I picked myself up, assessed the damage, and made my adrenaline-quavering legs start to work again. A short distance ahead was a checkpoint where I overheard spectators talking about moose and looked up to see two huge dark shapes wallowing in the willows, unaware of the human and equine drama unfolding on the road nearby. I was psychologically shaken and I wondered if I'd hit my head. Blood was oozing through my shirt from my shoulder. My legs now felt like they belonged to Gumby, and Laredo seemed more like Pokey than the burro that had taken the lead just a few moments ago. Over the course of the next few miles, I watched from behind as George and Jack gradually pulled away, and then disappeared out of sight. A couple hours later I finished a solid half-hour behind them in second place.

Just getting to the point where I'd taken that spectacular fall had required months of training and preparation, not to mention more than three hours of actual racing itself. In a split second it was over. I had won the race six times previously and at 52 years old felt as if my last chance to win another World Championship had just been literally dashed upon the rocks. I wondered how many races could possibly be left in me. Laredo, despite having won the race two times before, was also no longer at the top of his game. Besides, I had other major issues looming in my life, including a career in journalism that had become almost as big an anachronism as this crazy sport, and a son with autism. Back home awaited another year of scrabbling for a meager living, another year of struggling through each day of frustration, noise, tension and anxiety. And all the self-doubt and questioning that goes along with it.

૭

The heart of this story began eight years before. Mary had all the signs of early menopause. Her mother had gone through the change early at 44, and so Mary thought this was it. Well, she was right about the change, but it was a change of a different type. While on a get-away to Taos, New Mexico, for our anniversary, Mary was very fatigued and spent a lot of time napping. After returning to our home in Colorado, a pregnancy test showed a pink plus sign. We braced ourselves, as Mary had suffered four previous miscarriages.

We met as students at University of Colorado in Boulder on a blind date arranged by our roommates. She was in the prenursing program and I was in journalism. On the date we realized we were actually in some classes together — psychology and sociology. We agreed to meet up for class. We quickly became friends, then lovers and embarked on an intense and sometimes stormy relationship that would follow us through our entire college experience, and on into young adulthood. We held hands while walking to class. I was mesmerized by her lithe figure and easy-going nature. I wrote poems to her. We did almost everything together and enjoyed many of the same activities. We ran. We hiked. We skied. We fished. Later Mary would also take up pack-burro racing and win many races herself. In 1986 after a horrific accident in which Mary was dragged down a trail by one of our burros I suggested we get married. It was not the romantic proposal that she'd dreamed of all her life, though I actually was kneeling before her as she soaked her wounds in bloody bathtub water.

Like any relationship, over the years the marriage had been pushed to the brink several times. I believe much of this was due to my unorthodox lifestyle and career choices, coupled with my aversion to having children. My own childhood experience had been somewhat less than ideal. I'd watched our friends and family who'd had children and I'd seen what the stress of raising kids had done to their lives, their relationships and their freedom. In my opinion the world was clearly not short on people, and in fact it was overpopulated. So what, really, was the point of having children anyway?

Mary, on the other hand, had experienced a wonderful childhood filled with family and friends. She came from a large family with four brothers and a sister. She had been raised as a Catholic and children were always a big part of her dreams. As time went by I could see that having a child was something Mary wanted and perhaps even an experience she needed for her life to feel complete. We became more lax with the birth control. Each miscarriage came with a grief beyond words. Yet for me each one also came with a guilty and shameful sense of relief. It was almost as if the Universe was trying to tell us something, and was validating my aversion to fatherhood. When I would feel this sense of relief it would make me feel perfectly awful, and spin me into the depths of confusion and depression.

This time Mary did not miscarry, and the transformation over the next seven months in both her and me was profound. This period was also tumultuous time in which we lost two friends, one to cancer and the other to suicide. My mother was undergoing chemotherapy. And my work situation was in a state of flux, a situation that had become to feel all too normal. I was adjusting to the idea of fatherhood, something I'd run from all my life. Still, there was the joy of seeing a belly grow more plump, breasts more full. We started to think about names. Friends held baby showers. We moved the bedroom upstairs and my office downstairs, and repainted both. Time seemed to simultaneously drag and fly.

We visited a doctor in Colorado Springs who specialized in very high-tech ultrasounds. It was during the first appointment that we learned the baby was a boy. On the second visit the doctor pointed out a ventricle of the brain that appeared a bit larger than normal. But he wasn't sure whether this was just due to the positioning of the baby in the uterus at the time of ultrasound, and he also wasn't sure whether this had any implications for the child's development. Mary cried all the way home. For days she was distraught and insisted that something was wrong with the baby. She suggested that I should leave, that she would take care of the child. I reassured her that everything would be OK. That even the doctor did not seem certain or alarmed by what he saw, and that he also did not mention any possible problems if indeed the ventricle was enlarged.

I was much more apprehensive about the weather. The baby was due in mid-April, which really meant anytime between late March and late April. The previous year a storm that dropped 7 feet of snow had stranded us for five entire days here at our Wet Mountain homestead, which sits at an elevation of about 8,700 feet. I had actually enjoyed the solitude that storm provided, but now the idea of having to deliver my own child was daunting. I asked a couple of experts what I should do in that event and they both said "nothing."

The gifts and baby gear began to arrive. Mary's sister Janet visited to paint the bedroom, and while she transformed the walls to a pale orange faux pattern we discussed the importance to Mary of having a child. Janet conveyed to me the serious importance this was to her sister, that children were something they had been raised to expect, and that life could not be complete without.

Knowing that we were having a boy I began to think of all the things I'd missed out on as a child that I would make sure my son would experience. There were visions of teaching him about the natural world, taking him camping and fishing, and all the other things that fathers wish for their sons. Yet still there was the apprehension. At one point I remember lying on the floor of what was once my office and looking around at the newly painted room, the stuffed animals and books. The crib. I was 44 years old and I began to tremble out of fear and mourning for the independent life that I had known and would soon be leaving behind. Once again I felt that sense of shameful selfishness that somehow would not leave.

The due date came and went, and the weather turned beautiful. Birds began to arrive, including mallards, kestrels, mourning doves, robins, bluebirds and flickers, but no storks. Then on a sunny Monday morning came a sign, followed by slight contractions. We packed up our bags and headed to Pueblo, 50 miles east. A quick check at the clinic revealed that the baby was not arriving imminently, but the contractions continued. We went for lunch and then for a stroll on the Pueblo Riverwalk.

Another check that evening suggested that we should just head back to the ranch. I left the bags in the car and made dinner, a lovely poor-man's chicken Marsala. While we were cleaning up the kitchen Mary doubled over with a contraction. We started counting and timing. Then later we decided to go back to Pueblo, where at about 12:30 a.m. we checked into the birthing room at St. Mary Corwin Hospital. Mary was actually born in this same hospital nearly 44 years prior, and fresh out of nursing school she had found her first job there in the nursery.

The labor continued all night and into the next day. Mary's friend Wendy Raso, who is a certified nurse midwife, arrived in the morning and spent the entire day acting as a dula. Since Mary is a former employee of the hospital and knows a lot of people in the business of delivering babies, we had plenty of helping hands. By the time the moment arrived, we had Wendy, two medical doctors, a resident and two RNs in the room. Two more RNs, friends of Mary's from work, waited outside the door. I felt confident that if I were to have a heart attack while Mary was in labor there were enough medical professionals to handle it all in stride.

Meanwhile, I alternated between manning a damp washcloth and two cameras, one film and one digital. I had already come to terms with the idea of being a dim moon orbiting a very bright planet. Finally the delivering doctor said, "next time is going to be it." Sure enough, Mary pushed and a face appeared, much larger than I expected. There was a short delay and the shoulders squirmed out, followed by a shorter delay and then the rush of the child's entire body greeting the air. I had the presence of mind to lift my right foot just before a gush of amniotic fluid shot across the room toward my shoe. One must always stay a step ahead. There was a sacred moment of silence followed by crying. It was 5:04 p.m., April 20, 2004. His name was Harrison.

Quickly the team of medical professionals toweled him off and I was summoned to a table and handed a pair of scissors to cut the already crimped umbilical. I couldn't quite see through the maze of arms and hands, and frankly my hands were not all that steady, so it took two cuts to completely sever the cord.

Once the baby was in his mom's arms and things had settled down some, I quietly left the room. I went downstairs and out the front doors, then took off running down the street. I ran past homes and stores, motels, past a park. I ran out of sheer terror. I ran until I realized I really should get back to the hospital. And then I ran back.

Mary and Harrison had to stay in the hospital for observation for a couple of days. Meanwhile I drove home late both nights and back to Pueblo each morning. On Thursday we were discharged and brought our baby home, only to be greeted by the blizzard I had been dreading for a month.

It arrived pouring down snow like a summer rainstorm, and it probably would not have been any problem at all if Harrison were not slightly jaundiced, if his mother's milk had not stopped flowing due to engorgement, or if the electricity had not begun to flicker on and off. After living here a number of years I've learned that you can sometimes get the jump on a storm like this simply by moving vehicles from the house uphill to the gate. Late that night I went out into the storm and swept the snow off both the truck and the Subaru, and watched the lights of the house flicker through the driving sheets of snow. I marveled at how such a joyous occasion had suddenly taken on overtones of *The Shining*.

The power went out for real later that night. We resorted to formula, and Mary became an emotional wreck. I knew that we would have to leave in the morning. At first light I drove the Subaru the half-mile up our road to make sure we could get out to the main county road, then decided to "evacuate."

At this point there was about 18 inches of snow and the main road had been plowed one lane's width. It took a little while for us to get packed up and it just kept snowing harder. By the time we drove back up to the main road the plowed lane had a good deal more snow over it. The highway was still more than three miles away through open rangeland. The visibility and depth perception was poor, and on a big curve not far from the highway I hit a ridge of slush with the left wheel while driving a little close to the right edge. I was driving really slowly but we slipped off the shoulder and into a snow-filled ditch.

I tried digging with my hands and pushing but the car would not budge. Mary sat in the backseat with Harrison, who was resting calmly in his little baby carrier seat. I finally decided to start jogging through the snow to nearby Bear Basin Ranch for help. However, on the way there I ran into a neighbor in a truck. He had a tow strap and shovel and easily pulled us out and got us back on our way.

Next we found Highway 96 to be virtually unplowed. I had a very real pang of fear before descending Hardscrabble Canyon at 8 mph. It seemed to take forever to drive the 19 miles and 3,000 vertical feet to Wetmore, where the road conditions improved at about 6,000 feet, and where I chuckled when I saw a guy heading up the hill pulling a huge speedboat behind a truck. I breathed a very real sigh of relief as the first patches of black asphalt appeared through the slush.

The storm ended up dumping three feet of heavy wet snow and we camped at Mary's parents' house in Pueblo with Harrison on a photo-therapy blanket for his jaundice while neighbors braved the storm to feed our animals back home.

I decided to drive home Saturday morning to check on things and clean up. A few miles out from Pueblo I noticed a flock of seagulls circulating above the highway directly ahead of me, and also a minivan distant in the oncoming lane. I didn't think much of it until I became aware that something was awry with one of the gulls. It was flapping oddly and tumbling toward earth.

The gull landed right on the highway between our approaching vehicles, just shy of the minivan's side of the double-yellow line. The possibilities for omens were almost incomprehensible. I'd read of people who'd witnessed birds dying in mid-flight, but the timing in this case was a bit uncanny. I just wanted to get my child and his mother safely home.

The next day, Sunday evening, we came back home to settle in for real. The snow only took a couple of days to melt, and within a week winter had suddenly become spring. Mary's milk began to flow quite freely and Harrison's jaundice disappeared. The quiet realization that someone I loved more than anything now lived in my house began to sink in. One day, while cleaning the corrals, I heard a racket from the top of the big dead pine that stands sentinel over this place we call home. I looked up to see two kestrels mating upon one of the uppermost branches. Another omen from birds. I wondered if they knew what they were getting themselves into.

అ

My odyssey into the world of pack-burro racing began with a phone call back when phones still had cords. The voice on the other end of the line was pack-burro racing legend Curtis Imrie, whom I'd met through a friend, asking me if I wanted to go for a training run with his burros on the upper stretch of the World Championship Pack-Burro Race course. I told him "no thanks," but he said to call back if I changed my mind.

I hung up and thought it over for a few moments. Then I picked up the phone.

That quick and reckless change of heart changed everything in my life forever. In the years to come I would make major life decisions — things like careers and where to live — based on what was best for long-eared equines. Over these next three decades I'd train many burros, some of them wild. I'd win epic races on that course. More importantly, I'd establish a ranch-based lifestyle, cultivate some of my closest friendships and relationships, and learn more about myself, other people and animals than I could have ever imagined.

That first outing on the Fairplay course opened up an entirely new world to me. Most of the day would be spent with a burro named Moose above timberline, that line of demarcation where the high-altitude environment is simply too harsh for trees to exist. It was a day filled with clear blue skies, crisp thin air, sparkling reflections off snow banks that lingered right on through July, and clear cold snowmelt that poured over the rocks, seeking out the rushing streams. Bouquets of wildflowers sprang out of spongy turf that is green only a few weeks of the year. As we passed through that landscape marmots and picas — the small mammals that inhabit the alpine realms — made shrill noises. These sharp chirps echoed off the talus slopes that framed alpine views bigger than life itself.

And the burros! These wonderful animals. I loved how they moved through that high-mountain environment, smoothly and comfortably, confidently yet cautiously. It was as if they had been there before, or perhaps they could channel the collective consciousness of the hundreds of burros who had already passed this way before them with explorers, miners and, in more modern times, pack-burro racers.

This Colorado sport was conceived in 1949, just a little more than a decade before I arrived on the planet. With mining on the wane, promoters in the mining towns of Fairplay and Leadville saw a way to parlay local legend — in this case miners racing with their burros from the surrounding hillsides back to the courthouse to file a claim — into economic development. As a tourism attraction, they masterminded a race that was 23 miles from Leadville over 13,187-foot Mosquito Pass to Fairplay. Over this course, participants would race burros loaded with packsaddles that had to weigh 33 pounds and contain a pick, pan and shovel. The burros could be led or driven with a lead rope not to exceed 15 feet in length. No riding was allowed.

And from that first race with those basic rules — and a $500 prize from the *Rocky Mountain News* — a sport was born, complete with its own culture and history. Today there are commonly as many as a half-dozen of these events in Colorado each summer, including a Triple Crown, which comprises a 29-mile World Championship course in Fairplay, and a 20-mile course in Leadville, both of which reach the summit of Mosquito Pass; plus a 16-mile course in Buena Vista. Each of these courses offers up high-altitude scenery with healthy helpings of True West adventure. Over the years, I've run through heavy rain, summer snowstorms, blazing heat and I've been pelted by hail and awed by many lightning storms. I've experienced the many extremes and vagaries of equine nature. The rugged and rocky terrain is unforgiving, and I've been fortunate enough to survive some tremendous spills without serious injury, though I've witnessed entrants being taken to the hospital after falling, being caught in ropes and dragged, and even kicked. The natural elements also can get your attention. Once Curtis and I were training above timberline on the Fairplay course. A thunderstorm rolled in over the top of the Mosquito Range and we crouched on the balls of our feet to watch it pass. A bolt of lightning shot down from the black clouds then branched into several forks and illuminated the entire area with a purple glow. We looked at each other in wonder and disbelief, knowing no marmot, pika or ptarmigan could have possibly survived.

When I first started racing in 1980 an aging hardrock miner named Joe Glavinick was still among the top competitors. I've now been running in pack-burro races for about half of the sport's existence and have been witness to a transcendence of sorts. While the sport was fairly esoteric in those early years, a resurgence in its popularity has been sparked by articles in the mainstream media, a documentary film on the sport called *Haulin' Ass*, in which I am listed as "starring" as one of the three main characters, and the recent designation by the Colorado Legislature as the state's official Summer Heritage Sport. Today's shotgun starts are perhaps some of the most Western — wild and woolly — in my personal experience with twice as many entrants, many of them neophytes who are reinventing the sport with their own experiences and adventures.

☙

Perhaps my trepidation about having children was rooted in my own early childhood or the lack of it. And maybe it was also partly about the desire to recreate a childhood as an adult since I had not had much of one as a kid. My biological father was prone to drunkenness and abusive behavior. I remember way too much about him, and along with the blur of birthday parties and Easter egg hunts, many of my earliest childhood memories are quite unpleasant. . . . My father arriving home drunk in the morning, with the family car wrecked and spewing steam from the radiator. Suspicious wounds from bar fights. He once handed me a loaded revolver and I luckily escaped with my hand intact though burned black by a gunpowder blast. There was a cross-country move that I later learned may have been more about fleeing jurisdictions than it was about new jobs and a fresh start. He was abusive to my mom.

Once, on a hot and sunny day while my mom was at work, he left my sister Shelby and me in the car with the convertible top down while he went inside a bar and drank the afternoon away. When it was time to pick my mom up from work he emerged from the bar and proceeded to drive to her office. He was so drunk that he swerved through the traffic. While making a lefthand turn at a stoplight onto a river bridge, he drove up onto the sidewalk and crashed into the bridge railing. He simply and catatonically backed up and then continued on his way, at last arriving at the office and coasting very slowly downhill into the parking lot. That's when he decided to puke. He opened the door of the car as it coasted along and leaned out. My mom, seeing this unfold as she was walking down the steps of the building where she worked, dropped everything and began to run. The car bounced to a stop at a cement parking stop and he was hanging halfway out the door, his head lolling over a pool of his own vomit. Shelby and I were sunburned but otherwise uninjured.

I was afraid of my father and couldn't stand the way he treated my mom. One day he came home drunk again, and things started to go downhill as I had witnessed happening before. I was 7 years old and my memory is dim. Perhaps it's been recast by time and the inner workings of my mind. As I remember, I tried to intervene. During this fracas he picked me up and I kept struggling. He eventually lost his grip and dropped me. I landed on a coffee table and it smashed under my weight.

And that was it. If this was my first fight I didn't win it. But I had won a war. My mom picked me up, and grabbed my sister on the way out the front door. Over the next few days my father would pack up his belongings and leave.

In the next few months Shelby and I would receive birthday gifts through the mail, addressed to us from our dad — ceramic Disney character figures, Cinderella and Pluto, with accompanying wristwatches. They were packaged in clear plastic cylinders with the watches strapped to the round bases that fit inside. I don't know what became of the watch but for so long I remember keeping among my treasures this ceramic figurine of Pluto that I believed to be a gift from my father.

The term "single mom" had not really been coined yet but my mother heroically assumed this role. We were broke quite often as she struggled to pay the rent, purchase a car, and put groceries on the table. I remember one morning in particular watching my mom take a hammer to a glass piggy bank. Then from this, her actual life savings, she doled out some coins and sent me off on my bike to the store for milk. I left the grocery with the half-gallon of milk in a paper sack, and rolled the top of the brown bag around the right grip of my handlebars. On the first curve momentum swung the milk carton to the right and the bottom of the paper bag ripped open. The carton hit the curb with a splash. I got off my bike and sat there on the curb with my head in my hands, and watched the milk trickle away in the gutter.

We later learned the Disney watches were not sent by our father but rather on his behalf by some concerned relative of his. In fact I never heard from him again. I cruised along until I was 44, never fully realizing the meaning of his departure from my life and the damage he had done. And then Harrison came along. It wasn't until I had my own son that I realized how truly screwed up it is to leave your child behind this way. To not have any contact at all. To never know or even wonder how it all turned out.

A few years afterward my mom remarried to Dave, who took over the duties of fatherhood, and adopted both Shelby and me. He provided an important male influence, a more secure home life, and encouraged us to pursue educations. A range manager for the Bureau of Land Management, he sometimes took me along on his Saturday field duties near Las Vegas, Nevada, to places like Devil's Hole, where the endangered Devil's Hole Pupfish made their home. He also taught me the finer points of fishing, hunting, camping and other outdoor activities. We moved across the country with Dave's job twice, once from Las Vegas to Northern Virginia when he took a position with the Department of Interior in Washington, D.C., and then back out West to Craig, Colorado, the summer before my senior year in high school. After graduating from Moffat County High in 1978, I headed off to University of Colorado at Boulder where I enrolled in the journalism program.

❧

In those first pack-burro races I was just happy to finish. In fact, in my first race with Moose in 1980, I finished dead last, earning the "Last Ass Over The Pass" trophy. I had run a marathon and several shorter running races. But the burro courses are so rugged and so long, and the challenge of training both myself and a large animal to finish was immense.

Those early days training with Moose and hanging out at Curtis' Little Menokin Ranch near Buena Vista will always stand out as a period in my life when the world seemed wide open. That's what pack-burro racing represented to me then when I was out with Moose on the roads and trails around Curtis' place at the base of Mount Harvard, the third-highest mountain in Colorado at 14,423 feet. Curtis was in his racing prime, a serious contender, and on his way to winning three World Championships. I was taking it all in and learning as much as I could about training both myself and the burros.

Back at Curtis' ranch there often were interesting people hanging around. Curtis is an independent filmmaker and actor by trade, and some of the friends helping him with his productions had well-known names. Steven Peck, son of actor Gregory Peck, was appearing in and helping with filming Curtis' productions. Musician Norton Buffalo often was around — a harmonica player, who was so quiet, observant and soft-spoken you'd never guess he played with the likes of the Steve Miller Band, Bonnie Raitt and The Doobie Brothers. In addition to Norton's actual presence, Curtis always had tapes of Norton's solo harmonica music in his car and home boombox. Once Curtis arranged a concert in the local bar, The Lariat, in Buena Vista and I got to see Norton play in front of a rowdy crowd. His trademark harmonica riffs will always remind me of that time in my life. Norton died of cancer in 2008, and although I didn't know him all that well, news of his death and the resulting reconnection with his music brought me back to a time and place when everything good in life seemed to be laid out before me.

Also often a fixture at Curtis' ranch was his mother, Mary. She and Curtis' father, Walter, had bought the place with the dream of making it a summer retreat in the Rockies for their family. However, after Curtis' brother drowned in the nearby Arkansas River, Walter rarely visited the place. Mary would spend a few weeks there in the summer but they had largely abandoned it to Curtis. A strict Christian Scientist, Mary often quoted from the Bible and eschewed all modern medicine. She was a great woman and I learned from her the importance of having a sense of order to things, something she believed to be a plan of God, but something I seemed to adopt as common sense, and take to compulsive levels. To this day I still generally plan almost all daily, weekly, monthly, even yearly activities by an order. *This* always comes before *that*. I must get one thing done before I can move on to the next. That sort of thing. And I attribute it all to spending that short time spent with Curtis' mom.

There was an order to learning the ropes of pack-burro racing, too. The races traditionally paid prize money to 8th place, and eventually I found myself finishing in the money. From that perspective I could see the winner's circle, but it was 18 years, several burros — Moose, Jumpin' Jack, Clyde, Hannibal and Spike — and a multitude of hardships, before I put together a championship run.

彡

From the earliest beginnings it seems clear I was not cut out for the urban or suburban lifestyle. For the better part of 30 years, Custer County, Colorado, has been home, with 23 of those years in the Bear Basin Ranch area, about 15 miles from the small town of Westcliffe, and about 50 miles from the nearest sizable municipality of Pueblo.

Despite a development surge in the late 1990s, this area of the Wet Mountains remains relatively wild and open. Rolling hills of ponderosa pine, spruce, and aspen are offset by south-facing slopes where high desert flora such as yucca and cactus dot the landscape. Open parks, or meadows, stand between. On a regular basis I see herds of elk and deer, coyotes, bobcats, bears, the occasional mountain lion, and countless hawks, eagles, ancient ravens, and all manner of other small animals, birds, and reptiles. Some of the earliest of recollections here struck me with such awe that they are forever etched in my memory. That first summer early one evening I watched with my hands in soapy dishwater as a cow elk crossed the open meadow to the west to drink at the spring in the draw below the house. As the elk returned to the trees, where I guessed it must have had a calf hidden, it paused and let loose a huge spray of urine, sparkling in the low sunlight. One winter while out running on a cold blustery day I saw a missile-like object streak across the sky and followed it to where a golden eagle slammed into a raven sitting on a snowbank. The resulting impact sent a cloud of white in all directions. On a spring day I was jogging downhill on a trail when a strange brown critter ran across my path directly in front of me. The only thing I could think of was wolverine until it hit the trunk of a nearby ponderosa pine at a dead run and started climbing. I backed out carefully as I realized momma bear was probably watching.

Such recollections of life here blend into a collage of encounters with the natural world. A kestrel on a fencepost pulling at the breast of a fresh-killed horned lark during a spring snowstorm. Thunderstorms turning my pasture into a raging river. Pairs of mallard ducks arriving on a spring breeze shortly after the ice melts off the stock ponds. A herd of 150 elk splashing through sparkling snow crystals in the below-zero winter air. A bolt of lightning arcing overhead as a curtain of gun-metal gray fell across the landscape. A red-tailed hawk spread out against a blue sky at sunset with a waxing gibbous moon in the background. The buzz of a rattlesnake alongside the trail. A seven-foot snowstorm. A bobcat hunting rabbits in a pile of rocks near the house. Idyllic autumns that seem to last forever. Bears crossing open ground. Curious deer with their big eyes looking right into the living room windows. Countless neon sunsets that defy description.

In addition to its closeness to the natural world, I also liked this location partly because it seemed to be a place where little economic development could ever take place. By my way of thinking these places always turn out to be more livable and healthier environments. What I didn't bank on was so many other people adopting this same philosophy and trying to make a go of it here. The price of real estate was very low when we bought this property, and we could not even begin to think about living here at current prices, though we now pay in other ways like gasoline, heating fuels, time and social isolation. Still, all roads seemed to lead to this place.

I graduated from the University of Colorado's School of Journalism in the spring of 1982. The previous summer I'd been an intern at *The Pueblo Star Journal* and *Chieftain*. The powers that be there at the time were so impressed with my work ethic and skills that they proposed I move right into a job opening in the sports department, and finish my degree there in Pueblo at what was then University of Southern Colorado.

But I only had one year left at CU, and I was also at that point considering a double-degree in journalism and environmental conservation. My friends and family urged me to finish my degree at CU, where the sheepskin would theoretically be more valuable than one from a smaller school. So I went back to Boulder, where I found out I would actually need a fifth year's worth of credit hours to get the double degree. I opted to stick with journalism, and four days after graduation I was back in Pueblo, working on *The Pueblo Chieftain's* night copy desk. I actually had to drive back to Boulder on my first days off to move the rest of my belongings.

Pueblo had some merit as a place to live and work, but it was really hot there in the summer and pack-burro racing had given me a glimpse of life in the high country. From my new home in Pueblo I could catch the trail along the Arkansas River and access other trails near the Pueblo Reservoir. By now I had adopted a burro named Jumpin' Jack Flash and I could keep him there. And though this still wasn't the mountains I could at least *see* them from this side of the city. After two years in Pueblo a friend at work offered a house for rent in tiny Wetmore, 26 miles away at the foot of the Wet Mountains. I happily picked up my stuff, much of it still packed from the Frisco adventure, and moved again. It was February 1984, and I was officially a resident of Custer County.

I ended up purchasing that house in Wetmore through a program that helped low-income people buy homes. It worked out fairly well as a base of operations for many activities I enjoyed. I was training for marathons back then, running burros, trail running, and cross-country skiing. And I could get to work at *The Chieftain* in an easy no-traffic half hour. When Mary and I married in 1986 we both were working evening shifts

— she at St Mary-Corwin Hospital — and we could carpool to Pueblo.

My relationship with *The Chieftain* took many strange turns over the years and I quit there once again in 1988 over a disagreement with the managing editor. My plan then was to make a living as a graphic designer and writer. This worked out fine for the first few months but then times got lean and I began looking for work elsewhere. There was a stint as a lumberjack on a trail crew at Devil's Thumb Ranch near Fraser where I traveled to work and camped while Mary stayed back in Wetmore. Then I signed on as editor and general manager of the *Leadville Herald-Democrat,* and we both moved to Leadville for 10 months, renting the house in Wetmore to a family who said they wished to buy it. I was able to board my burros in Leadville, but it was not nearly as convenient as having them right where I lived.

While in Leadville, I spent much of my free time driving around Lake County looking for a place to set up home with my burros. I never found that place and when word came that our renters had vacated the Wetmore house and left it in serious disrepair, I knew I could not afford rent in Leadville and a house payment in Wetmore. So I quit my job with the newspaper and we moved back.

As luck would have it, I found myself back at *The Chieftain* part time, and then a temporary opening for a full-time adjunct professor at The University of Southern Colorado soon appeared, and I still had some freelance work. We cleaned up the house and did some remodeling. And began to look for a place with more land. I was determined to not move again unless I had a place both for us and our animals.

There were some properties in the Wetmore area, but after living in Leadville, none of them appealed to our montane expectations, including a 10-acre lot right outside town and a 35-acre mountaintop with a view of Pikes Peak. Both lacked houses and would require building. We traveled back up the Arkansas Valley, looking at real estate in Buena Vista and Salida. But prices had risen faster than wages, and there was the question, as always, of where I would work. As a registered nurse, Mary always had options. But for me the opportunities were scarce.

We began to look at properties closer to home. In the Westcliffe area there seemed to be a bigger selection of newer homes on acreage, and, though a longer commute, these were still within driving range of Pueblo. We had actually begun working on a contract on an A-frame log house near the old mining town of Rosita when a friend who was also looking at real estate suggested we look at a property he'd visited on larger acreage. It was a small house with a barn, garage and 35 fenced acres located near Bear Basin Ranch for $91,000. We posted a For Sale sign in front of the Wetmore house and four days later sold it to the pastor of the church. We moved into the place near Bear Basin in May 1991.

At first this seemed like living right on the edge of the wild. The house was four miles of dirt road from the nearest pavement. The surrounding ranch land was Open Range, so we had to keep our gate shut to keep the Bear Basin horses out. But there was a tradeoff — the ranch had miles and miles of trails and we were welcomed by our new neighbors Gary Ziegler and Amy Finger. There were few other homes in the area, and we were at the end of a cul-de-sac road where there was just one other house. To the north was a large virtually untracked cattle ranch. Over the years that ranch was subdivided. Homes were built. We suddenly had neighbors. But the landscape in its unforgiving way remained much the same, wild and wide open.

҂

The realization that something is very different about your child sinks in slowly, even more so for fathers. At first there are subtle signs. Sensory issues. Sleep disturbances. Screaming fits that seem to last forever. Fascinations with things that spin. Lining up toys. The failure to meet major developmental milestones. Walking delays. Language delays. Issues with spatial awareness. "Echolalia" — repeating words or sentences like a parrot. "Darting" — running away with no referencing or regard for surroundings. Problems with "transitions" from one place or activity to another. "Stimming" — repetitive activities such as spinning toys, opening and closing doors, or making sounds like throat clearing. You tell yourself this is just typical for some kids, and that he'll grow out of it, and when others close to you point out these peculiarities it only steels your belief that time and the child himself will prove them all wrong. Then one day you suddenly notice the stark differences between him and other kids his age, like these differences had been invisible to you all along. The realization is not unlike the feeling you might be drowning.

Then other repetitious behaviors kick in, fascinations with things like patterns in floor tiles and carpeting, stairs and elevators, and opening and closing doors. Toilet training went on into Harrison's fourth year with many accidents before he finally learned to go to the bathroom when he needed to. Many times this happened in less-than-convenient locations — like at the school playground after the doors were locked leaving no access to the restrooms.

Typically moms notice developmental delays first. Mary, being a nurse and very aware of developmental stages, began to suspect issues early on. Fathers on the other hand tend to deny this, or argue that it's not what's happening, their notions further supported by reassurances from some friends and relatives who point to a kid who didn't walk until a certain age and turned out to be just fine, or tell stories about how they didn't speak until age 5 but still turned out to be a surgeon, or would eat only white bread and peas but turned out to be a talented film actress.

Autistic kids are famous for having eating issues. Temple Grandin for example mentions her problems with certain foods when she was young. Harrison also had eating issues. He would gag on foods with certain textures and was lazy at chewing and swallowing. Twice when he was little he choked on food and I had to quickly remember the baby Heimlich Maneuver from First Aid classes I'd taken years ago. I'd thought I'd never need to know this procedure, but when your child is choking and can't breathe, instinct and memory kick in quickly. I recalled the instructors saying that with small children there was a certain force that's just enough to get the food loose but not hard enough to crack a rib. Both times it seemed an automatic response when I realized Harrison could not breathe. Now I have images of chunks of food popping loose and flying several feet onto the carpet — and the adrenaline rush that followed — to accompany my First Aid training.

There were other sensory issues as well. Early on when Harrison began to walk, if he stumbled and put his hands out to the ground he often reacted as if he'd just touched an electric fence. It could be soft grass, dirt, gravel or even snow, but the reaction was always the same, a look of shock upon his face followed by loud screaming. When he was young he would not wear gloves of any type. A loose string in a sock could cost you an entire morning with screaming and tantrums.

The possible role of vaccinations in autism is a huge and emotionally charged controversy with scientific studies linking and then refuting the link. I can only speak from my own experience, and I do believe certain vaccinations may have played some part in Harrison's autism. Harrison had been meeting all developmental milestones until shortly after receiving shots around his first birthday. A few days following the vaccinations, a combination which included the MMR vaccine, he spiked a high fever during a vacation trip to Taos, New Mexico, and Mary began to notice some developmental issues afterwards. I am no medical professional, but my feeling is that in these children there's a "perfect storm" of multiple vaccinations, genetics and environmental factors that lead to autism. The fact is nobody really knows for sure, and the clear cause of autism may forever remain a mystery.

Mary is a courageous mom who realized early on that something was not typical with Harrison, and, despite my protests, sought out assistance. What seemed like an endless parade of therapists were invited into our home through a local agency. We were visited by a speech therapist, an occupational therapist and physical therapist. A young woman who is an occupational therapy technician began showing up at our house regularly to help with things like teaching Harrison to eat on his own and to "use his words." Often after these sessions Mary would become despondent and at night I would wake up to her sobbing.

Once a psychologist arrived to administer a battery of tests and while doing so started using the term "autistic-like." This behavior is "autistic-like." That behavior is "autistic-like." Harrison walked past him and the psychologist said, "See that. He walked by me like I was just a piece of furniture — that is an autistic-like behavior." Mary was struggling to hold it together during this session and I finally interrupted the guy and asked him to lighten up with his use of "autistic-like." Still, he continued on. He sat Harrison at the end of the kitchen counter in the high-chair, placed a plastic bunny out of his reach and handed him a pencil. Of course Harrison was supposed to use the pencil as a tool to reach for the toy but he did not — he just sat there in his high seat looking at the bunny. This also was "autistic-like." However, I'd already seen Harrison use spoons as tools to retrieve things that were out of his reach so while the psychologist was making notes I told him this. He finished with his note-taking then looked up at me and asked me to not interrupt because it was interfering with his testing. I felt angry at being scolded like this in my own house and in front of my family. It wasn't until thinking back on this many years later that I understood this anger was also fueled by my slowly dawning realization of the cards that we'd been dealt. Right then my inner cowboy just wanted to toss the psychologist out the front door.

❧

The word *burro* means "donkey" in Spanish. Donkeys, like horses and zebras, are members of the equine family of animals. The male donkey is called a "jack" and the female is a "jenny." Many people confuse donkeys with mules, which are the resulting hybrid when a donkey is crossed with a horse.

The first burros were brought to the New World by the Spanish, who used them to freight gear during colonization of Central and South American, and later expansion into North America. In fact, the Spanish outpost of Taos, New Mexico, was established, likely with the help of burros, in about 1615 — five years before the Pilgrims landed with their three ships at Plymouth Rock. Later in our history King George of Spain gave as a gift to U.S. President George Washington two large breeding jacks. These donkeys were the foundation stock used to produce draft mules that furthered the development of the new country and its expansion westward.

Donkeys are sturdy and hardy beasts of burden, known for their abilities to endure hard work, and do so on less feed and water than a horse. They have tough feet and can traverse rugged, rocky country and maneuver in tight spaces where horses and mules have more difficulties. When gold and silver were discovered in the West, prospectors chose these animals as companions to carry their gear into the deserts and high mountains where they hoped to find their fortunes. Some prospectors struck it rich but far more did not.

When the mining booms went bust many of these miners simply turned their burros out to fend for themselves. Some of these animals simply hung around the mining camps looking for handouts from those who had stayed behind. In the deserts of the Southwest, burros reverted to feral, forming wild herds in the open lands of California and Arizona. Today these wild herds are protected by federal law and are routinely subjected to roundups in order to reduce their numbers and prevent overgrazing and other damage to these fragile desert rangelands. Many of the burros in burro racing today are adopted former wild burros, or are descendants from burros that were captured from the wild and domesticated.

On a windy April day we went for a walk. Harrison's fourth birthday was in a few days. We walked out the driveway and down the road to a gate into the neighbors' property where I have permission to hike. When we turned around the wind was now in our faces and it seemed even stronger, peppering us with dust and sand. Harrison began to object loudly and to throw a tantrum. I picked him up and carried him on my shoulders for a short distance which calmed him down somewhat. Then my ball cap flew off my head. I had to set Harrison down in order to chase down the cap which was still rolling along the ground. Once I had retrieved it

I walked back to Harrison and lifted the shrieking child onto my shoulders once more, only to have the cap blow off my head again and have to repeat the same drill. This time I tightened the fit before placing the cap back on my head. For nearly four decades I had been free, within reason of course, to curse out loud, and so with a screaming child on my shoulders when the cap flew a third time I went through considerable vocal contortions trying to keep "goddammit" from leaving my lips. Unfortunately I only managed to keep it just under my breath. I felt badly for this slip-up but hoped Harrison was more concerned with the wind than my language. Since he was prone to echolalia and did not repeat it right away, I figured it was probably OK.

The birthday presents had arrived and so when April 20th rolled around we got out the video camera and set the gifts out on the floor for Harrison to open. He went about opening the packages with gusto, ripping the paper and smiling at each one. I especially wanted to get a video of him opening the gift from my parents, and so when he started on that package I zoomed in. As the paper peeled away to reveal a big yellow tractor, he beamed with joy, looked up at the camera with a huge smile, and happily exclaimed in his own precious little voice: "Goddammit!"

ॐ

Over the years I have trained and known many burros, like myself some more and some less employable. The first burro I actually owned, Jumpin' Jack Flash, was wild off the range and when he was finally trained to the point at which the unpredictable wildness was out of him, I missed that spirit more than I appreciated his newfound tractability. Next I had Clyde, born in captivity of wild parents. I ran all my fastest times on the pack-burro courses with Clyde, and won my first race with him. But he never had a World Championship in him despite finishing second a number of times. I trained another wild burro named Hannibal. There was a tame burro named Virgil given to me by a rancher friend. Then along came Spike, who finally won for me a World Championship, and then three more titles. I bought two burros, Billy Sundae and Ace, from breeders in New Mexico, a jack named Redbo from Curtis, and another jack named Laredo, with whom I won two more World Championships.

There were others as well and all of these burros had their own unique personalities. Some were runners out of pure joy and some were not. Some had a work ethic and others didn't. Some reached down deep in their hearts when the going got tough and others simply gave up. There really is no stereotype with burros just as there is no stereotype with people. As I worked with more and more burros I began to appreciate their individual qualities, and to realize that we're all here for a purpose. We're all on our own separate journeys, and in my journey I've found parallels between working with burros and parenting an autistic child. For sure no burro gets up in the morning and thinks, "Dang, I think I'll run up a 13,000-foot mountain pass today." Likewise, no autistic kid gets up in the morning and thinks, "I think I'll conform with societal norms today." The real key to success with either burros or autistic children is extreme patience and allowing them to find their own way. Each are unique individuals and one cannot exert command over them with good results. Only when they believe something was their own idea do they truly excel.

In this regard the sport itself has become a metaphor for life for me. Success at burro racing is both preparation and then literally dealing with what the world and an unpredictable critter throws at you on race day. Rarely does everything go perfectly. Sometimes things even go quite badly. It's how you handle what happens and go with the flow that determines success, whether that means winning or merely finishing some days. That's how life works, too.

Once Harrison's developmental delays had been identified, we were encouraged to seek out as many varied therapies as possible, and also to enroll him into preschool early to help develop more social-interaction skills. We began to hear phrases like "on the autism spectrum," and "Relationship Development

Intervention" (RDI) and "Applied Behavioral Analysis" (ABA). Mary bought books on the subject and signed up Harrison for everything she could find in the area.

We took him to RDI in nearby Cañon City for a few sessions. During one session the dysfunctional interaction between Harrison and the therapist was so painful for me to watch that I felt like it was almost abusive for us to subject our child to it any further. The therapist sat with him on a bean bag chair, and attempted to play a game in which she handed him a ball and then he was supposed to hand it back to her. He simply refused to participate and screamed. It seemed to go on for an eternity and I wanted to just say "stop it now" and take him away. I felt frustrated that we were spending our time on this. Finally the therapist simply gave up. Ultimately we decided to bail on that program.

Before Harrison was even 3 years old we enrolled him in early preschool in Westcliffe, where teachers Charlotte Havey and Terry Eiland welcomed him into the program along with his paraprofessional, Karen Gourley, who we called "Mrs. G."

It's a 15-mile trip to the preschool. There were days when I would drive Harrison there in the morning, then drive back home to do my work and get in some training. Then I would drive back to the school in the early afternoon to pick him up and drive him to Pueblo for speech therapy at Children's Hospital where Speech Therapist Jaclyn Mutz helped Harrison to make great strides by incorporating speech therapy with social skills lessons. By now we'd had some difficulties with Harrison striking out and also darting was becoming more common. Jaclyn was masterful with incorporating into her speech lessons "social stories" about why he shouldn't hit people or run away, and she often would make a little book with pictures and the story written out. When the session was over, we would drive back home, 145 miles of driving in all.

Once during the preschool years Harrison disappeared right out the front door of the school. The preschool was a big open room with lots of toys, equipment and activities going on. There was a hallway from the front door to the kitchen and two doors in the main room. Mrs. G simply thought Harrison had gone one direction when he had actually slipped out the front door. While she searched frantically for him inside the preschool, he crossed a side street and walked over to the salon where he usually got his hair cut. His hairstylist, Karalee, found him knocking at her door asking for a haircut and stickers. She was leading him back to the preschool as the general alarm sounded. For days afterward Karen apologized over and over, but I told her not to beat herself up over it. I knew exactly how easily this could happen. Harrison was quick and he really didn't know or understand anything about danger. We'd already had several close calls with him. Twice I remember catching him just before he ran out in front of moving vehicles. And once he disappeared from the house while Mary was vacuuming and I was out running. I was returning from the workout when I encountered her a half-mile up the road where she had caught up to him with her car.

All the while I continued to battle with the use of the label "autism." After all, no medical doctor or professional had ever told us that Harrison had autism. And in fact two medical professionals had told us they didn't think he was autistic. Finally a trip to Denver's Children's Hospital made it official. It was one of those early spring mornings when the gray clouds hang low like fog and the snow falls softly only to melt upon the roadways. A trip to Children's Hospital is a sobering experience. The place is quite large and busy — almost like a small city unto itself — and you will see kids bald from chemo treatments, others in Radio Flyer wagons trailing feeding tubes carried by their parents, moms and dads sitting in waiting rooms while their kids undergo heart surgery, small children with forearm crutches, burn victims, kids with Down Syndrome, other kids with autism both more and less severe than Harrison's, and kids with health problems you can't even see . . . hundreds of kids and none of them are there for the glass elevator, the artwork, the toys in the waiting areas or the aquariums with brightly colored fish. You think you have big problems but the truth is a lot of other people do too, and many of them have worse problems.

The assessment required a full morning of tests and evaluations. I remember in one of those tests the doctor blew up a balloon and then released it into the air, watching as Harrison tracked the balloon with his eyes and then walked over to pick it up. My eyes met the doctor's and she knew exactly what I was thinking, that his reaction to the balloon was typical.

"A typical child would bring the balloon *back* to me," she said, looking right through my doubt.

After it was all said and done, we were called to her office where the doctor, whom I am sure had faced other skeptical fathers before, looked right at me and said: "It is autism."

What I have come to learn is that the word means so many different things to so many different people, and the symptoms are so variable and come in so many different degrees. Though I had originally bucked the use of the word "spectrum" it actually is more on-target.

Once, early on, when I explained to a young woman that my son has autism, she asked, "And what does that mean, exactly?" Having been so close to the subject my initial reaction was one of shock. After all, hadn't she heard of autism? It's in the news all the time, and movies ranging from *Rain Man* to *Temple Grandin* have approached the subject. Yet when I really thought about it, her question was actually one of the most intelligent I've been asked on the subject. I still have no simple or definitive answer. While autism is a medical diagnosis, doctors don't really know what it is or what exactly causes it. There is no concrete medical test such as a blood test, chromosome analysis or brain scan to determine if a person has it. And unlike most other conditions, autism has a wide variety of symptoms and a wide range of severity in all people it effects. There are many stereotypes that are supported in popular books and movies, but not all people with autism have all of these traits.

Despite resisting the label for so long, I found a certain comfort in it. It provides a one-word explanation for how Harrison is different from other children his age, and gives us something to pin it on when he behaves oddly in public. Beyond that, the label is really meaningless. Just a one-word "explanation" for a person who has speech and communication issues, behavioral problems, is prone to being loud and screaming, and tends to fixate on repetitive behaviors.

In perhaps what is my own form of repetitive behavior, over the years I've traveled to the Mosquito Pass summit countless times — at least 70 times in races and many more in various training runs, sometimes twice in one day. This high pass, the highest drivable route in North America, received literary description in Wallace Stegner's Pulitzer-winning *Angle of Repose*. In the early frontier days it was the main route between the mining camps of Leadville and Fairplay. Father Dyer, the "snowshoe preacher," traveled the pass with God's word and the mail. As often as I've run up and down this pass, there's been something different and yet something the same about each trip. In races on this pass I've found the finish line with eight different burros. I've finished last. I've finished first a few times, too. In some ways I think my fascination and captivation with the sport was my response to the absurdity that life itself has always seemed to me. But over the years the thing that has impressed me most about my trips up and down Mosquito Pass is that they have provided a stunning backdrop for a life filled with wonder, magic, change, and difficult challenges that seem to come from out of the blue. If anything, these trips up this pass have served to cement lessons in winning and losing, triumph and tragedy, despair and hope, and even life and death. And for much of this journey I could not have known that this sport and these animals were in fact teaching me the arts of patience and perseverance that I would need later in life as the parent of a special needs child.

"Graduation" ceremony for Harrison's preschool will always be remembered as a day of infamy. The kids rehearsed a couple of days before the event and made little graduation mortarboard hats as a craft activity. Before we knew it, the big day had arrived. Early in the ceremony I could already see that Harrison was having a difficult time sitting still. But Karen, his paraprofessional, was managing to keep him in his seat. When the other children sang a song, he sang along with them — and without them — and also embarrassingly broke into other songs altogether.

Then the children filed out for the procession. As they shuffled back to their seats with their hats, it was clear that Harrison had somehow broken the mortarboard part away from the band and Karen was trying to put it back together. I was still hopeful and turned on my camera for the big moment. Certainly Karen would have to accompany him to the podium to get his "diploma" but I was ready to get the momentous photo. But Harrison began to get more unruly and loud. We laughed nervously but it made us uncomfortable. I wondered how many of the other parents were even more uncomfortable than we were. Finally he slipped away from Karen and headed for the audience looking for his mom. Mary held him for a while but his outbursts became more disruptive and so she finally carried him outside.

I sat. I didn't want to cause more disruption, and I was hoping that perhaps Mary would at some point bring him back inside.

I learned early in life that when your last name begins with "W" you always get to bring up the rear of things, and of course his name was the last to be called. The teachers looked around the room and then at me. The other parents were silent. All I wanted to do was take a picture, like the other parents did, of my kid getting his preschool diploma. But now I had to speak out to a quiet room full of people.

"He was being disruptive so she took him outside" was the only thing that came to mind. I turned my camera off and sat quietly as the ceremony ended.

Meanwhile, outside, there was a very upset little boy who really didn't understand why he had been removed from the ceremony, and an even more upset mom trying to come to terms with why her child sometimes behaves like this.

The day-to-day challenges posed by autism are invisible to most people, though sometimes the public gets a glimpse like this. For parents, there's only acceptance that often things don't turn out like you think they will. You learn to live with that fact. You move on and hope for a better day.

Living where we live it's difficult to not take in some wonder nearly every day, like the chance sighting of a bald eagle, a badger or a wild turkey. Early on as Harrison grew bigger, more mobile and more aware, we began taking nature walks on our property. Each spring the pasque flowers, which are wild crocuses, are the first to brave the cold. On those early hikes Harrison would walk through the pasture, bending down and touching each lavender pasque flower he saw and announcing, "flarrer, flarrer." The ponderosa pines, small and large, he touched lightly and said "tee, it's atee."

I remember kneeling beside an ant pile with him and watching the tiny red insects do their work. It took some effort to get Harrison to recognize the ants moving in and out of their entrance, but once he took notice he stood and watched intently as the ants went to and fro on their business. It was a tiny world he had never considered.

And then he was off, running through the brush, falling down, picking himself up, and taking off again. He cannot be caged. Not then. Not now. No kid large or small should be.

Long before I learned Harrison has autism I had the dream that he would share my passion for working with burros. I imagined him riding, exhibiting animals in shows, and going on backcountry pack trips. For me this was my vision for blending fatherhood with the lifestyle I'd known so long. It seemed only natural I would want to share that with my son, and it would also help provide a vehicle to the backcountry where I reconnect with my inner soul.

In the beginning I merely set Harrison on the burros bareback, then in a saddle for very short periods of time. Then we let the burro walk for a few short steps with me leading the burro and Mary spotting Harrison in case he might fall. Then we went a little farther each ride. Eventually we began taking rides from our home out onto the trails on neighboring Bear Basin Ranch.

During all this I read Rupert Isaacson's *The Horse Boy*. In this story, Isaacson finds a connection between his autistic son, Rowan, and horses, and the calming effect of horseback riding. So he took him to a place where both are still an integral part of life — the backcountry of Mongolia. The resulting story is compelling on many levels. For starters, the story is an epic real-life adventure. However, what struck home for me was Isaacson's familiar description of his son's speech habits, peculiarities of behavior, screaming, and tantrums. Most valuable was the manner in which this father openly discusses his very personal feelings about his son's condition, and the impact it has had on every part of his life, including his own physical and mental well-being, his work, lifestyle, and relationships. It seemed the only place anything could go right for Rowan was on the back of a horse, though Isaacson also describes some scary experiences that seem to come with the territory when dealing with equines. Isaacson ultimately takes his son Rowan on a epic backcountry horseback journey to visit a shaman in Mongolia in hopes of healing his son.

While I knew the idea of a horse trek into the Mongolian backcountry was likely not in our cards, it occurred to me we could replicate the concept right here. Harrison already was riding our donkeys and we have access to some of the most amazing mountainous backcountry on Earth. Perhaps one piece to this autism puzzle had been right here under my nose all along.

The positive therapeutic effects of riding for people with brain disorders are well known. There is a difference between therapeutic recreational riding and actual "hippotherapy," which is done under the guidance of a licensed therapist (speech, occupational, physical, psychologist, etc.). But we don't need no stinking badges — as Harrison rides we often sing, recite books, and point out the different types of trees, wildflowers, and animals that we see along the way.

Donkeys seem well suited to this task since their movement is virtually the same as a horse, yet their generally calmer nature makes them less scary. They are less explosive and less likely to run away. And most are shorter than horses, so if there were an accident it would be less distance to fall.

We noticed right away that on the days when Harrison rode, and even on days following a ride, there was marked improvement in his disposition and behavior, and fewer tantrums. The activity was also therapeutic for us as parents — actively engaging our child in an enjoyable activity while freeing ourselves to hike and enjoy the outdoors. We led the donkey from the ground and kept a watchful eye out for any safety issues, such as wildlife, horses, or our dog crashing out of the brush.

In the years B.C. (before child) we always made a point of getting out for a pack trip with our burros at least once each summer. Usually we chose the cloudless days of late August or September to avoid the monsoon season when severe thunderstorms could wreak havoc on a backcountry trip with downpours and lightning.

Harrison's arrival in 2004 put pack trips on hold, but the summer after he turned 3 Mary and I thought perhaps it was time to get out again. Then we thought about it some more. What we really needed was a solid kick in the butt. Some friends were planning a three-day trip into the backcountry in late August so we rudely invited ourselves — and our 3-year-old boy — along for the adventure.

Even with the big mountains in plain sight, it can be a daunting project to actually pack into them for an overnight stay. For years I kept all the gear packed — just add food and we were basically ready to go, with tent, sleeping bags, cooking kit, and all the other necessities. However, it must be noted that when you have burros to carry the freight, the term "necessity" can take on an expanded definition to include such items as folding camp chairs, thick foam mattresses, full-size pillows, ice chests stuffed with real food, a bottle of red wine, etc.

As we began to gear up for this trip, however, it was clear we would have to pare back. We'd only be able to take two burros because we'd need the flexibility to manage Harrison. We planned to have Harrison ride one of our animals some of the way, and also carry him in a child backpack over some of the rougher and steeper sections of trail. This meant we'd have only one packer to carry all our food and equipment.

We chose Spike as Harrison's riding burro because he's generally unflappable on the trail, and because he has the lowest center of gravity. We bought Harrison a helmet and began practicing, taking him on rides from the house out to the trail. Truly it was more challenging to keep the helmet on Harrison than it was to keep Harrison on Spike. For the most part he seemed to enjoy riding and quickly gained an uncanny sense of balance in the saddle.

For the packer, I chose our biggest and strongest burro, Redbo. I knew he could carry a good deal of weight and he needed the work anyway. Plus, if I wanted to go riding from camp once we got there, he was large enough for me to ride. Once the animal situation had been decided it was just a matter of gear. Years of disparate use had left much of our equipment widely scattered. The sleeping bags were stowed away all over the house, having been used for couch-camping during many sleep-deprived nights when Harrison was a fussy baby. Other gear, like the tent, was lost somewhere in the shed, where the packsaddles and panniers also were hanging covered in a fine layer of dust. One day I hauled all of this gear outside, spread it on the lawn, hosed it off and left it to dry in the sunshine.

We had decided upon the Upper Sand Creek Basin, now part of the Great Sand Dunes Upper Preserve, as our destination. It's one of my favorite places, and the best camping is at lower elevation in that valley making for warmer nights and mornings. We'd avoid the crowded Upper and Lower Sand Creek lakes and instead head down the creek to make camp. From there we could do a day trip either up or down the trail.

I spent almost the entire afternoon prior to the trip packing and getting ready, and the next day we were at the trailhead well before the rest of the group, and actually had our burros saddled and loaded when our friends pulled up with their trucks and trailers.

Joining us for this trip were Amy Finger and partner Gary Ziegler from Bear Basin Ranch, neighbors Pete and Nancy Hedberg, and Carl Batson and Lorie Merfeld-Batson. All would be riding horses and each couple also had a packhorse. Since we'd be traveling slower managing the two burros and Harrison, we decided to get a head start on the procession and headed on up Music Pass with Harrison riding, myself leading the burros and Mary "spotting" Harrison. I had my eye on the gathering storm clouds.

On this day Spike's work ethic left something to be desired. He was slow and caused us a few problems as we tried to keep the two animals moving while also spotting Harrison from alongside. Harrison rode a good deal of the way up, but we carried him over the steeper sections, finally arriving at the Music Pass summit, 11,395 feet elevation. We stopped to admire the view of Tijeras Peak, and I recalled a backcountry ski trip to the top of this pass with Mary's brother Alan many years before. We took photos then began our descent into the Sand Creek Basin. When the trail grew less steep, with less of a sidehill, we put Harrison back on Spike and made good time downhill to the lefthand fork in the trail that heads down the valley. While surveying one potential camp, and noticing the scarcity of firewood and level ground, we looked up the mountainside to see the rest of our party crossing Music Pass, appearing like ants topping out on the summit in the distance. We decided that since we had some lead-time we'd scout farther down the trail for a better camp. At one point a spring was pouring shallowly over the trail and as Mary led Spike through this wet section of trail Spike decided to jump over the water. Harrison bounced out of the saddle, onto Spike's rump, and then luckily right into my arms. We acted like it was no big deal and then went right back to looking for a camp.

But we didn't find one and turned around in time to meet the group just below the first campsite. It was by now early evening, and the camp took shape in short order. Quickly the tents were pitched, a kitchen tarp was raised over the campfire area, firewood was gathered, and horses and burros were put out to graze. Though the clouds were still building, there was nary a sprinkle.

Harrison found all of this quite amusing, especially the tent, where he enjoyed rolling around in the sleeping bags, and playing with the door and window zippers for quite some time. Then it was out to the campfire, where he ran around in circles, spilling people's drinks, getting in the way of the cooks, and in general having a grand time. By the time we turned in for the night he was truly zonked out, snuggled between his mom and dad in the best goose-down sleeping bag we own.

I awoke about 3 a.m. to the rumble of thunder. It was a good distance off but as I lay there listening as the thunder grew nearer. I unzipped the door and stuck my head outside, watching as the flashing thunderstorm marched quickly north to south along the eastern edge of the San Luis Valley, just behind an unnamed peak to our west. I zipped the door back up and started to drift off to the sound of the creek as the storm drifted off in the direction of the Great Sand Dunes on the other side of the range.

Moments later I was awakened by more thunder. A new storm cell seemed to be headed our way. Soon the thunder grew close and the tent was lighting up like a lantern with each strike. The rain pelted the nylon then became a steady roar. The seconds between the booms and the flashes told me the storm was not directly overhead, but the light show was nevertheless unnerving. All through the storm I lay awake thinking about how a little lightning display like this never used to shake me up terribly. I thought about Harrison bouncing out of the saddle earlier that day. Suddenly I had the realization that I had brought my 3-year-old son over an 11,000-foot pass deep into the wilderness, far from the "safety" of civilization. If anything bad were to happen I would never be able to forgive myself. I had sworn I would not allow fatherhood to change who I am, but somehow it had done so when I had least expected it.

Meanwhile Harrison slept soundly through the thunder.

The next morning we gathered around the smoky campfire to compare notes. The only person who'd gotten much sleep was Harrison. Pete and Nancy's tent had leaked and some of their gear was wet. While we were drinking cowboy coffee and eating pancakes, sausage, and eggs, the thunderheads were regrouping, and I learned later that I was not the only one thinking about bailing.

But Amy and Gary were not among the frail-hearted. They were already planning a horseback ride from camp to Milwaukee Basin at the northern headwall of the valley. I aired out the tent and sleeping bags and watched the weather. Oddly, the wind began to blow, shredding the clouds and leaving behind a perfect bluebird day. Mary offered to stay behind with Harrison, so I saddled Redbo and went along with the horse-riders.

Oddly, so did Spike.

At first I thought he would follow for just a while and then stop to eat, or that he would go back to camp. But every time I turned around, there he was, ambling slowly along behind us. The problem with this was that Redbo was waiting for him rather than keeping step with the horses. So, my horseback friends waited from time to time for us to catch up. When we reached steeper sections they didn't need to wait as much, and when we walked out below the headwalls of the Milwaukee Basin cirque, Spike was still plodding along behind.

We ate lunch there, and then Amy and I rode back to camp ahead of the others. I turned the burros out to graze and quickly shifted from riding to fishing. Harrison had been playing in the creek just up from the camp and I had noticed some fish in the pool just above there. I caught and released several smaller cutthroats while my boy splashed in the water and threw rocks. Despite the commotion, I could see a much larger fish in the pool.

I had just about given up on this big cutthroat when quite lazily the fish took the fly and the entire pool seemed to erupt in slow-motion splashing. Mary was close enough that I called for her to get the camera. With Harrison wading around beside me I brought the fish to the bank. Mary snapped a photo and then I turned the orange-red trout, about 20 inches, back to the stream. It was the biggest fish I've ever caught in these mountain waters. I fished the creek downstream for quite a ways that afternoon, catching and releasing dozens more cutthroats but none were even half the size of this fish.

At some point downstream the creek became walled by cliffs and difficult to fish. So I cut through the brush a short distance to catch the trail back to camp. This trail parallels the creek downstream several miles to the

Great Sand Dunes. As I was walking along, I noticed in a stretch of softer dirt some burro tracks headed downhill. At first I had some difficulty getting my mind around this. We hadn't been down the trail this far with our burros. Soon I realized that either someone else was traveling with burros — not likely — or my burros had gone on walk-about. I hid my flyrod in the brush and started down the trail, stopping from time to time to make sure I still had tracks to follow. I've known of horses that have been lost in these mountains. A few are found alive. Some are never found at all.

I kept expecting to see Spike and Redbo ahead grazing the grass along the trail, but the tracks kept leading me downhill. I knew the trail crossed the creek several times so I hoped to catch up to them at one of these fords. But when I reached the first creek crossing I found a pathway into the water lined with willows, a muddy bank, and no burro tracks whatsoever.

I walked in circles from the last place I'd seen tracks. Already my mind was spinning with thoughts of packing Harrison in a backpack back over Music Pass to the truck, leaving most of our gear behind, and coming back with another burro to search fruitlessly for my lost animals. It struck me that if I did not find the burros this evening that I might never see them again. Finally I found the hint of a track in some dirt, then a smashed aspen leaf. There was a faint trail leading through the forest, roughly paralleling the creek.

The path was little more than a game trail and it meandered through aspen groves and meadows with knee-deep grass. There were no tracks to follow on this lush ground and I was merely working on instinct. I found a hidden outfitter's camp tucked away in those woods. Onward I walked.

Then, finally, in a grassy glade I looked ahead to see Redbo looking back up at me in the early evening light. Spike was standing nearby with his head down in the grass.

We were now a good distance downstream from camp. I had no rope with me so I couldn't lead them back. The only option was to try to drive them and hope I could loose-herd them ahead of me back to camp. The going was slow until we made it back to the trail. But soon the burros got the idea and trotted ahead of me all the way back to camp.

Our last evening was splendid and dry, and there was good food, drink and even music around the campfire. We had a tense few moments when Pete and Nancy's horses wandered off from camp, but they were found in fairly short order, and soon we were all snoozing to the lyrical rush of Sand Creek.

The next day we packed up and made the uneventful trek back over Music Pass to the truck. We were backcountry travelers once again. Harrison was now one, too.

As time went on we began to combine riding excursions with fishing expeditions into the Sangre de

Cristos and the Wet Mountains. These treks reopened the world I knew so well before Harrison was born. The rolling stretches of trail, the flash of trout, the aspen glades and the old spruce-fir forests all came rushing back into my consciousness. It was all still there for me to relearn and for Harrison to experience with a fresh and open mind.

There were trips to the Swift Creek beaver ponds, where Harrison caught his first fish with a flyrod, and to the Goodwin beaver ponds, where we realized we had left a segment of the fishing rod back at home and therefore could not fish. We took a much longer excursion into the Macy Lake drainage. But a high point was when Harrison rode Redbo to Horn Lake and back, 11 miles and 6.5 hours total. I was totally amazed at how my son rode that steep, rocky, slippery trail, and also how well Redbo took care of him even when we were caught in an icy downpour of rain and hail on our way back down the mountain.

As the school year began, the days grew shorter and the weather turned cold. Riding became less frequent, and it seemed like Harrison's behavioral issues were increasing. On a warmer fall day I decided to get him out for a ride. I suppose I should have been expecting a setback. We stopped at a neighbor's and were watching 4-H kids practicing with their horses in the arena. Harrison was on Spike, and I was on foot and had the lead rope. Harrison had been protesting his helmet. He cantankerously removed it and dropped it to the ground next to Spike. The burro didn't even flinch.

I picked up the helmet and just a few moments later glanced at Spike. People who spend considerable time working with livestock, particularly equines, sometimes can tell when all hell is about to break loose, and I suddenly had the realization this was one of those times. In a split-second I saw something very wrong going on in Spike's eyes, and I was later thankful for the tiny jump this gave me on the situation. I still have no idea what had spooked Spike. But what happened next unraveled so fast it took me days to piece it all back together. Suddenly Spike backed, spun and took off bucking. The next thing I knew I was sprinting down an embankment, "climbing" the lead rope hand-over-hand as I ran trying to gain control of the berserk burro, who was running away with my son and bucking like a saddle bronc.

At some point I knew I had to somehow get a grip on Harrison and pull him out of the saddle before the whole rodeo got away from me. But this would require both hands and letting go of the rope. I remember getting my left arm around Harrison and pulling him off Spike just as I let go of the rope and lost my footing. For what seemed like forever, I wrestled horizontally in mid-air, flying, twisting, and contorting in an attempt to hit the ground first and break Harrison's fall.

We landed in some shallow snow that had collected in the shade of a tree, and miraculously nobody was seriously hurt, though Harrison apparently bit his cheek, my hand was bleeding from rope burn and I felt both physically and mentally beaten. I held the screaming boy tightly and offered up a prayer of thanks that he was OK.

All the magic of the connection between animal and child can come undone in only a few seconds. And then the second-guessing sets in: Is this riding thing really helpful, or is it merely my ego at work? Is it just too dangerous? Spike was a "dead-broke" burro and had suddenly turned psycho. I was reminded of my first horseback riding experience when I was about Harrison's age. A Shetland pony ran off with me at my great uncle Glenn's farm in Missouri. I have a dim memory of the pony running fast across a pasture and stopping short of a fence. I heard then for the first time — and it's something I've heard many times since — that little voice inside that says, "Hang on. Don't let go!" Somehow I stayed on. When I visited the farm shortly before Glenn's death in 1997 none of the landscape seemed familiar, but that ride remains forever in my memory. Over the years I've heard that same voice saying "Hang on. Don't let go!" when life has taken me for some wild rides, both figurative and literal. And I realized I had heard it again as I struggled to gain control of Spike when he took off with my son.

We were able to convince Harrison to get back on a different burro the next day, and he rode Redbo for a short ways. There was no problem with him keeping the helmet on.

"Spike is bad behavior," he said from the saddle. "Redbo is better."

From that moment on we decided Harrison could ride our other burros but not Spike. Redbo, Ace and Laredo were all good rides and we'd focus our time on them and hope that we didn't have another scary episode like that.

But things tend to happen when you least expect them. Harrison had come down with the Chickenpox early in the Spring the following year. He was not really that sick, just itchy, and so one sunny evening we decided to take him on a short ride. We chose Ace and struck out toward the Bear Basin trails. We were walking slowly along with me leading Ace, when I felt something happening on the other end of the lead rope. I'm still not sure whether Ace stumbled, stepped in a gopher hole or had sort of hopped to the side a bit. Whatever happened, when I turned around I saw Harrison in slow motion sliding headfirst off Ace's left flank with his arms stretched toward the ground.

Harrison immediately went into screaming and crying mode and we could not get him calmed down. He was holding his arm, and because of his communication difficulties we could not understand what he was feeling or experiencing. We made it back home and I began to worry as he would not stop crying. I wondered if something might be broken in his arm.

I finally called the clinic in Westcliffe. The clinic was closed and there was a message directing folks to call the sheriff's department in case of an emergency. I called the sheriff and they took down my statement about what had happened and said they would have someone from the clinic call back. I waited and shortly the phone rang. It was the nurse practitioner from the clinic and she said to meet her there as soon as possible.

On the drive there we explained to Harrison that he would have to be calm and that they would take an X-ray of his arm to see if there was anything broken. He seemed to calm down and when we got there he cooperated with the medical workers as they took the X-rays from various angles. These X-rays revealed a "buckle fracture" in his wrist, obviously from when he had put his arm out to catch himself when he took the dive off Ace.

They could not do anything for Harrison at the clinic other than to give us a CD with the X-rays and suggest that we get him to an orthopedic specialist within the next few days. On the way home we stopped to watch two young foxes play along the road in Silver Cliff. Harrison acknowledged the foxes and I knew everything would be OK.

Back at home I spent the rest of the night and evening trying to calm down and think about what to do. In the morning I called my old friend Dr. Robert Hamilton and explained what had happened. He said to email the X-ray images. When he called back he said he would be speaking to an associate of his, Dr. Dave Walden at Premiere Orthopedics in Colorado Springs, and would get back to me. More importantly, Doc Hamilton gave me a little bit of a pep talk that I really needed at that moment. He said that while I might be traumatized by the accident at the moment, when it was all said and done this entire episode would prove to be a growth experience, as Harrison would have to learn to cooperate through the process of more X-rays and getting a cast.

On Monday morning the phone rang and it was Dr. Walden's secretary. She knew all about Harrison, his autism and his chicken pox. She said to bring him right away and to call from the parking lot — they would open a side door so we could avoid the entire waiting room scene. I got Harrison packed up as soon as possible and called Mary who was working in Pueblo so she could meet us in Colorado Springs.

If I weren't already thankful enough for the help from Dr. Hamilton when I got to the office there I was even more so. While waiting on further X-rays I looked over the walls filled with autographed photographs from professional and Olympic athletes of all types, all of them thanking Dr. Walden. Harrison wasn't just seeing an orthopedist. He was seeing one of the very best in the country, plus getting special treatment by the office to boot. They gave him a choice of colors and we left there with him sporting a purple short-arm cast.

The accident curtailed Harrison's riding for some time and left him scared of getting back in the saddle. It also brought to surface my own issues of self-doubt. Was riding really all that helpful for Harrison, or was I just using this as some way to make sense out of the lifestyle I had created? However, true to Doc Hamilton's words, the entire experience also marked a tremendous leap forward in Harrison's development. It took some time for him to regain his confidence and trust in a burro again, but within a couple years we had him riding again, though to this day he seems to prefer to hike along and let the critters carry his lunch and gear.

≈

From early on one of Harrison's repetitive behaviors was opening and closing doors. It began with small doors like those on cabinets and appliances, and it grew to include doors to vehicles and homes, and even to large commercial doors at businesses. In the early days he would open and close doors in the kitchen. Sometimes he would open a number of doors, say a cabinet door, the dishwasher door, oven door and refrigerator door, some part way, some all the way, then stand back and look at them from various angles. He actually trashed the clutch in the washing machine by opening and closing the door so many times while it was running, causing it to stop and start abruptly. When he began to focus on larger doors, he also became interested in the moving parts, particularly the "door closer" mechanism found at the top of so many commercial and institutional doorways that pulls the door shut on its own.

Once just before Christmas Harrison and I went to the Westcliffe post office to mail out the holiday cards. The post office is a fairly harmless place to let Harrison run around while I take care of business. The only way out is the front door and there's very little trouble he can get into.

I had most of the cards already stamped and just needed a few more stamps before dropping the cards into the slot. I figured I'd be in and out of the post office quickly as it was about to close. Then the cashier noticed the square shape of the envelopes and informed me that they would all require additional postage. I bought the additional stamps and went out of the lobby to a counter where I could add stamps to all of the cards.

At first I managed to get Harrison engaged with helping me put the stamps on the cards. But he quickly grew bored with this, and then I employed him to run to the mail drop with cards as I stamped them. On the way back and forth he managed to help a few other postal customers — some of whom knew him — post their holiday mail.

Because of his fascination with doors big and small the mail drop held his interest. He also went with a few customers to collect their mail from post office boxes, which also have doors, and some allowed him to get their mail out and hand it to them, and to open and close their boxes. Most seemed cheery about having a happy 4-year-old boy help them with the Christmas mail.

I had just finished stamping the last envelopes when an older woman walked into the post office and Harrison followed her back to her postal box. I got the idea she was not as amused with this as the other customers. As I was headed back to fetch him, Harrison managed to push the lady's mail all the way through her box and back out onto the floor behind the wall. The woman was not pleased and as I picked him up to carry him away he threw a bad tantrum, screaming, kicking and slapping me about the head. The post office was now closed for business, but I managed to knock on the door and get the attention of one of the kind workers there to retrieve the lady's mail.

But as I left, I heard out loud from the old woman what I would begin to realize people were thinking as the next few years unfolded. "You better watch out. I'm an old grandma," she said sternly as she walked out the door. The implication being that she didn't put up with brats.

To that, Harrison threw himself screaming and kicking onto the floor. Another fairly smooth outing had just turned into an embarrassing drama. What the old lady had no way of knowing is that Harrison isn't a brat and that I really have little control over his behaviors. And in what turned out to be a scene that would repeat itself over and over in the years to come. I had to pick him up and carry him out of the post office kicking and screaming.

ॐ

In 1998, after several second-place finishes at Fairplay, I finally put together a championship run with Spike, who after 29 miles nosed out Oscar and my friend and fellow competitor Rob Pedretti right at the finish line, winning the 50th running of the race. With the *Outdoor Life* Network filming the entire event, Rob and I reached the summit together, exchanged places all the way down the boulder-studded pass, and ran neck-and-neck over the last 12 miles of the course, arriving finally to a showdown on Fairplay's Front Street. When the race came down to a finishing sprint, it initially appeared I might walk away with yet another second-place disappointment. But then something clicked and Spike shifted into another gear. There was a split second in my life when time literally stood still. I gave Spike a little push and his nose crossed the finish line just ahead of Oscar's.

There had been many people in the burro-racing crowd who believed I would never win a championship. I took it upon myself to prove to them all that it was no accident. Spike and I won again in 2000. And then in 2003 and 2004. In 2005 I won again with a burro named Laredo, putting me in a handful of just four people who'd won three championships in a row. In 2007 Laredo and I found the finish line first again.

Then came the long period that seemed like the inevitable downward decline, with one disappointment after another, including second-place finishes so heartbreaking I nearly retired from the sport fearing I was beginning to appear like some defeated prize-fighter or aging quarterback who just didn't know when it was time to quietly go away.

But through it all I still loved being in the game, and I was still competitive. I still loved the high country, the animals and the lifestyle they had taught me. What impressed me more and more as time went by is how this sport helped me to reconnect with my deepest feelings, my wildest dreams. Winning a race is great but the thrill fades quickly. What you learn about yourself in the process stays with you for a lifetime.

One summer day Harrison changed his name. He simply decided to be "Chad" rather than Harrison. How he decided upon the name Chad he would not say. There was a boy named Chad in his class, so perhaps that's where he had heard the name, though school had been out for a few weeks. We went along with it for a few days. But it was difficult. If we slipped up and called him Harrison by mistake he would throw a fit. From what we could understand he had decided he didn't like the name Harrison.

This was truly disappointing. We had chosen the name Harrison after weeks of discussion and careful consideration when Mary was pregnant. Mary's due date had been April 15, and a work associate of hers had suggested the name Harrison in honor of the Beatles' George Harrison who wrote the song "Taxman," which appeared on the group's 1966 album *Revolver*. This name seemed to have promise. I noted that the start and finish of the Leadville pack-burro race was on the town's main street, Harrison Avenue. For years I'd been a fan of author Jim Harrison, who wrote *Legends of the Fall* among other great books. And Harrison Ford conjured up the image of Indiana Jones. When no better name materialized, Harrison it was.

One of the problems with suddenly changing your name to Chad is that not everyone in your immediate community gets the memo. And so for a few days as we went about the business of life we endured screaming and fits whenever someone addressed Harrison by his real name. Finally we talked it over with him and decided that a better solution than Chad would be to shorten his name to Harris. He was agreeable to this. And Harris was actually an option Mary and I had previously discussed if Harrison proved to be too many syllables. We tended to name our animals with one-syllable names because it's easier for them to process, and in case we need to blurt out the name in a hurry or when oxygen-deprived. We would gradually get the word to friends and family and slowly change his name to Harris.

He was Harris for about one day. And then he announced that his new name was "165."

165?

"Yeah, that's my number name."

My first thought was that One-sixty-five has more syllables than Harrison.

We asked how he chose that number for a name and he refused to answer. The only thing we could figure is that he was also very much interested in signs at this point in time and there was a sign for Colorado Highway 165 nearby.

Soon 165 also began to pass out number names for others. Dad was 164. Mom was 199. His friend Mara was 111. Her mom Monica he called "20-Zoo." For his birthday his friends Max and Alex gave him a T-shirt with the ironed-on numerals "165." He gave number names to some of his other friends at school and to some random adults, including cashiers in the natural foods store we frequented. He would walk up to total strangers in public places and announce, "Hey, your number name is . . ." and then he gave them a number. These numbers, whether random or not, were never duplicated. They seemed to be cataloged in his memory. Weeks later we would see someone who we had infrequent but regular contact with and he would call this person by this number name. I began to suspect that he was visually indexing images of faces with these numbers in his brain. Perhaps somehow this helped him to keep people straight in his mind.

Once in the natural foods store, a woman who was there shopping took notice of 165 and struck up a conversation. I explained the number name concept. It turned out she was a psychologist and had worked with autism-spectrum kids. She offered that his use of a number name was his way of making sense of his own recognition that he was different than other people, and that it was his way of coming to terms with the fact that he didn't really like it.

The first part of this unsolicited psychoanalysis was fine with me. The second part not so much. You get what you pay for, and I had to wonder what sort of psychologist offered up such free therapy to complete strangers in grocery stores.

For many, many months Harrison continued to use his number name. When being introduced to people for the first time or when someone would ask him his name he would mutter quietly and quickly, "My number name is 165." He insisted on using 165 on name tags, on the screen at the bowling alley or wherever he could substitute numbers for his real name. Some of his teachers were not real thrilled by this. One day we were leaving school and he was dragging behind. I walked past a Jeep with an older woman behind the wheel, probably waiting to bring her grandchildren home from school. I was nearly to our car when I turned to see where Harrison was. Suddenly I realized he was pounding on the passenger window of the Jeep. Before I could respond the woman rolled the window down and he yelled to this complete stranger: "Your number name is 467!" Then he turned and ran to the car.

∾

Burros of course are not well known for their cooperative nature, so motivating one to travel at a quick pace over 29 miles of mountainous terrain may seem akin to teleportation. The general public regards donkeys as "stubborn," while many of those who work with burros prefer to attribute this to the "cautious" nature of donkeys, and their tendency to stand their ground rather than flee like a horse when spooked — a notion that does not give donkeys the intellectual credit they rightfully deserve. Over the years working with donkeys, horses and mules, I have formed my own opinions based on the fact that I have known horses as stubborn as any donkey, and donkeys as tractable as the average horse. If there's any truth to the theory of stubbornness, it lies in the fact that donkeys are generally smarter than horses and even some humans, and their independent nature tells them they do not necessarily have to do whatever is asked of them by people. They are also smart enough to make some unwitting humans believe they are being cautious when they are actually being stubborn. Moreover, all equines are individuals and like humans some are more agreeable and tractable than others. For example, as a human I do not think that I am particularly agreeable or tractable, a trait that has left me, as one friend put it, "unemployable."

~

When I was a kid I nearly drowned. I was fishing alone, and walked across a shallow spillway, slipped and fell into the lake. It was a scary plunge and though I didn't know how to swim somehow I got myself out of the lake. My mom signed me up for swimming lessons the next day at the YMCA.

Since I had this experience I felt it was important to introduce Harrison to the water as early as possible so that he could learn to swim without any fears. We hired Lisa Kaufman, a certified swim instructor at Club America in Westcliffe, and I began to take him to the pool on a regular basis. Harrison is a slow learner when it comes to physical activities. He does not take instruction easily and seems to prefer to learn by watching others. This is how I taught him to cross-country ski. However, swimming is quite different — a person could drown trying to learn. So Lisa had the difficult task of teaching him this life skill and I always admired her patience and perseverance even when after months of lessons Harrison still was not properly swimming, though he had learned to dog paddle and glide underwater a short distance with his head down.

Taking Harrison to the pool was always an adventure. His curiosity about the doors and locker doors and combination locks would always take over his attention, making it difficult for him to focus on changing into his swim suit and showering before entering the pool. Also he was always quite loud in the locker room, where voices tend to echo off the walls and tile floor. The pool, heated partially by a solar system, was not particularly warm, especially during the winter months. So when he got out he would run shivering for the hot shower. Then when told to get out of the shower he would scream, protest loudly and refuse. When at last I would turn the shower off he would scream some more. And then once he was out of the shower his fascination with the lockers and doors would take over again, while I encouraged him over and over to get dressed. I always felt bad for the other guys in the locker room, and also battled with my own embarrassment and levels of patience.

After one summer lesson he was running around outside while I spoke with Lisa about his progress. Suddenly he tripped and fell right on his face on the cement. The impact with the abrasive cement cut up his nose, the area beneath his nose, lips and mouth. The screaming was almost unbearable as we took him back inside to clean up the damage as best as possible. It echoed in the open room of the pool. He continued to scream all the way home, a 25-minute drive in an already noisy aging Subaru Forester.

భ

Over the years I have struggled to put words to the screaming, shrieking and other noises, that Harrison often makes. Is it enough to say it's loud? That sometimes it seems a constant in our lives with few intermissions? That it's grating, like fingernails on a chalkboard? That often — especially in the morning — it can make me believe there are steel marbles rattling around inside my hollow cranium? That there are times it is so startling I completely forget what I am doing, and so distressing it renders me perfectly useless for hours? That sudden outbursts have nearly caused me to lose control of the wheel while driving?

How does one spell those sounds? Those screams? That screeching? How does one explain the ridiculous phraseology that makes sense only in the context of years or months of background and experience with this person? Or that sometimes makes no sense at all in the context of anything I can determine? It's almost like speaking an entirely different language, or vernacular, only one never really becomes fluent.

For some time Harrison referred to himself in the second person, and often phrased statements as questions. For example, if I were to ask him what he had for lunch, if he answered at all, he might say. "Did you have a sandwich for lunch?" This meant "I had a sandwich for lunch." This is just one example, and after a while a person begins to pick up on these peculiarities of communication.

He can also be as repetitious as a CD stuck on replay, asking the same question over and over again even after being given the answer, or even when he *knows* the answer. Sometimes the answer is not to his liking and he'll scream loudly, then ask the question again, as if the answer might change because he protested, or merely because he'd asked it again.

Screaming is actually just part of life around here. Often, upon awakening, Harrison reacts by screaming. Sometimes this is in the middle of the night and accompanied by slamming of his bedroom door. Many mornings, upon awakening, anything he feels like protesting — eating breakfast, the battery running low on his iPad, being told not to scream, get dressed for school, whatever — he protests with noise. Over time this noise has a tendency to scramble a person's brain. Often I lose focus of what I am doing. At times during meals the noise has been so unbearable that I've picked up my plate and gone outside to eat by myself at the picnic table, with only bluebirds, robins and Eurasian collared doves for company.

ॐ

If you are the parent of a child with autism, perhaps nobody personifies hope as iconically as Temple Grandin. She's autistic but is a university professor and has designed many humane livestock handling facilities in the U.S. If you work with animals, Temple Grandin offers a picture of how animals see things. And if you are someone who may be on the "neurodiversity" spectrum yourself, Temple Grandin helps provide meaningful insight. The movie about her life, *Temple Grandin*, won five Emmy Awards in 2010. She also has written several books, including *Animals in Translation*, *Animals Make Us Human*, and *Thinking in Pictures*.

I'd read some of her books and had always been struck by the way she was able to put words to many things I had learned about moving and handling livestock, including donkeys. A person who learns to see things the way animals do develops a manner of approaching them, and also starts to look ahead for things that may spook them, like a flapping flag or a glint of light — animals notice these details separate from the overall picture, while most people only see a "generalized image."Animals also react strongly to motivating factors and to fear factors — it's easier to work with them when they are motivated. In reading Grandin's books I realized that I had already arrived at many of the same conclusions and techniques, but had just never put these into words the way she does. Even more compelling was what Grandin had to say about autism from the perspective of someone who had excelled in life not only in spite of, but actually *because of,* her different way of viewing the world around her.

When we learned that Grandin would be speaking at the Buena Vista High School gym we made plans to go, and on that afternoon we headed out with Harrison on the 174-mile round trip up and down the Arkansas River to see her talk. On the way to the lecture there was a "WIDE LOAD" vehicle approaching along the curvy U.S. 50 Arkansas River canyon road, and the driver of the truck traveling ahead in our lane hit the brakes suddenly. I in turn hit my brakes, and that's when Harrison lost his lunch. I pulled over at the first pullout along the Arkansas River to assess the vomit damage. We suddenly realized we had not brought a change of clothes or wipes, and we had precious little time before Grandin was to begin her lecture, "Autism, Animals and Visual Thinking."

The first thought was to just turn around and go home. But then I realized the Salida Wal-Mart was closer than home at this point. At least we could get a change of clothes, a cheap towel to fashion a makeshift booster chair cover, and something to clean up Harrison and the car. After a pit stop there, and some food from a local restaurant, we headed on to Buena Vista and soon found ourselves in a packed gym well before Temple took to the stage.

Grandin's entertaining sense of humor caught me totally by surprise. For example she described the autism spectrum as including a wide range of people from those who are non-verbal to Einstein — "and half of Silicon Valley." Later she described "geeks, nerds and Aspergers" as being the same thing, and referred to diagnosing autism as "behavioral profiling." Though she professed to taking a low dose of Prozac herself, she expressed disgust at the wholesale use of drugs to treat autism, and suggested instead that parents consider sensible dietary adjustments and more exercise to help their children.

Grandin stressed the need for more participatory learning opportunities, as opposed to theoretical, to give those with different minds an opportunity to learn. She said it's disappointing schools have stopped offering classes in subjects like sewing, autoshop, welding, and other vocational programs that allow students to actually learn to make or do something. She thinks this has carried over into society at large and it concerns her that the work force is becoming less and less capable of making and fixing things. She also mentioned that our education system focuses much too hard on students' weaknesses and not enough on their strengths. I couldn't have agreed more.

All the while Harrison was running amok in the hallways, checking out doors and stairs. I had gotten myself wedged into a seat in the packed bleachers and I felt badly that Mary was having to pay more attention to Harrison than to what Grandin had to say. There was a point during the lecture when Harrison broke away and ran out onto the gymnasium court where Grandin was speaking and up to the podium. She turned and looked at him and then took a few moments to collect her thoughts as Mary rushed out to retrieve him. I wondered if she could tell or if she wondered if he was autistic.

A few moments later she was discussing sensory issues, and mentioned something she called "slow attention shifting." She used the interruption caused by Harrison as an example — "Like when that little kid ran out here a few minutes ago" — to demonstrate how when her train of thought is disrupted it takes a while for her to get it back on track. Ironic as it was that Harrison provided the example, I realized as soon as she said it that I too have this issue. When I get interrupted while talking, working, or cooking, it can be very difficult for me to regain my focus for some time. I believe it takes me much longer than most people to get back to the task. Sometimes an interruption can lead to another interruption, and another, ultimately costing me an entire day.

One of Grandin's books, *The Way I See It* is largely about visual thinking. She sees things in pictures. As an example she offered Van Gogh's "Starry Night" (one of my favorite paintings) as a visual thinker's interpretation of some rather complex mathematics. Verbal communication, she says, tends to cloud some ways of thinking. As we drove home that evening I could not help but dwell on something else that Grandin had said. I actually thought it was her best and most interesting quote of the lecture. She said: "When you're weird you have to sell yourself." The statement brought cheers from the crowd. I thought about all she had been through to get to where she is today. How it'd worked out for her despite her weirdness. Maybe there was hope after all. For Harrison and for all of us.

᠕

In the summer we regularly go to the Westcliffe Farmers Market. I served on the board that hosts the market, and many of the farmers and vendors at the market know me and Harrison, and generally welcome him there despite the occasional disruption. One such Thursday Harrison's second-grade teacher, Leanne Stover showed up to buy fresh vegetables from the Family Roots Farm table.

Harrison has had problems in the past processing when he sees people in places where they are out of context to him. For example, he'd see another kid from his class at the park or grocery store and would freak out. It was as if he could not process that these people could be someplace other than where he normally sees them. This has improved over time. Now he sometimes just covers his eyes and laughs in these situations. So I was caught by surprise when Leanne said "hi" to him and he went berserk. He screamed, flung himself down, pulled his hat over his eyes and started yelling loudly and crying. "She's a stranger. I don't want to see her." It went on for what seemed like an eternity but was probably only a few minutes.

The incident caught me off-guard, and I didn't really know how to react. Leanne was totally calm. Harrison had been a student in her class the previous year, and she was well aware of his unpredictable nature. While she went about making her purchase of vegetables from the farm stand and then went on her way, Harrison continued to scream and throw himself about, finally ending up behind one of the vendor's tables, sobbing loudly on Rubbermaid containers of honey and lotions. When I tried to comfort or help him up, the uproar only rose again. In the end I could only wait until he had recovered somewhat and then lead him away from the scene in embarrassment.

Despite the regularity with which these situations arise, I always seem taken by surprise, and to never have the presence to react properly. I think later that I should have apologized publicly to Leanne and everyone else present, or that I should have immediately picked Harrison up and carried him away. These are the things that always seem to enter my mind after the fact.

CHAPTER 2

FOURTEEN YEARS AFTER that first World Championship in 1998, I spent the last few warm weeks of the late summer and fall soul-searching and questioning another run at the Fairplay race. Who could know what would have happened if I hadn't taken that tumble up on the pass? But it seemed like if I wanted to make another serious run at it I was going to need a different burro. George was 10 years younger than me, unquestionably a faster runner at this stage in my game, and with the race months away he was already the odds-on favorite. Plus, I was simply exhausted. The rigors of fatherhood and the challenges of autism, compounded by the struggle for the all-mighty dollar had taken a toll. The only chance I might have was with an animal that could outrun his. Curtis had an idea for me to run a jack burro named McMurphy that he had, and we worked out an agreement. Then one day he called and told me that sadly McMurphy had died unexpectedly. It seemed I was getting all the messages, and some were even coming from above. Then one fall day Curtis contacted me with a rambling message that I would initially dismiss the same way I did the very first time he had called me so long ago. This time it was by Facebook rather than land line, and three words stood out: "Boogie for Fairplay."

꙳

For several years I've taken Harrison to weekly piano lessons with Phyllis Bishop, a retired music teacher in her early 70s. Since she began giving Harrison lessons, she and her husband Don have become some of my favorite people in Westcliffe. I feel like they are family. I typically run an errand during the half-hour lesson, usually arriving back to listen to the end of the lesson, and Phyllis often takes the lesson beyond 30 minutes. I am extremely thankful for Phyllis' patience and willingness to accommodate Harrison's learning differences as she teaches him to play on her polished black baby grand piano.

One day during the lesson I just went for a short drive through the valley's country roads, then made a loop back to town. I arrived back at the Bishop's and took a seat on a lawn chair in the Bishops' sunny front yard. Very soon Phyllis came out the front door and said "OK, I guess we won't have a piano lesson today." I could hear frustration in her voice. I walked up to the porch and she sat down on her bench and then she began to tear up. Harrison had refused to play his songs, wouldn't cooperate in the lesson at all, and then just started screaming. She had become frustrated, then decided to just call off the lesson. I felt terrible. While I was out driving around, she was going through all this. I talked to her for a while until she seemed OK and then we drove home.

On the drive I thought how experiences like these have a way of taking me to rock bottom. I must be strong when I am weak. Get up when I fall. Accept each moment as if I chose it, etc. I know there are people in this world who suffer far worse, have much bigger problems . . . I am not a whiner, not a quitter. It was the silly season when people put up signs in their yards urging us to vote for this person or the other. There was a new sign that had appeared in front of a neighbor's place along the road to my house, like so many others, a flimsy vinyl tarp-material sign on two stakes. I looked to see who these neighbors were supporting because I know our political views differ but this message was not political.

I'm not a religious person. I consider myself "spiritual but not religious" and all that . . . part Zen, part Pantheist, sorting through what I think could be real about any of the mainstream religions, but really just mostly confused. I don't really even know what I think God is. The sign said simply: "God Loves You."

For some reason I found that message comforting on my way home.

∻

My professional life it seems has always been sort of a high-wire act without any sort of a safety net. I originally went to work for the Star-Journal Publishing Company back in the summer of 1981 as an intern-reporter for the *Pueblo Star-Journal*. Though I had worked at some small newspapers in Colorado and even had toured the *New York Times* as a high school student, I was somewhat overwhelmed by my insertion into what was then a vibrant two-newspaper operation, with the *Star-Journal* publishing in the afternoon and *The Chieftain* coming out in the morning.

I was taken under the wing by a middle-aged guy who though competent had a tendency to tell elaborate tales about things like singing in a band with Linda Ronstadt and being trained by Indians to track mice across granite. At the end of my internship I was distracted by talk of a position in the sports department, with the idea that while working I could finish my degree at what was then the University of Southern Colorado. With journalism jobs as rare as they were even then, the opportunity was tempting, but I opted to return to the University of Colorado in Boulder and finish my degree. The following May I graduated from CU on a Saturday and started work on the Chieftain's copy desk the following Monday. Thus began my tempestuous history with the newspaper. After resigning in 1983 to start a newspaper in Frisco with my friend Miles, I left again to take an open-ended three-month leave of absence in 1985, then returned to ascend to management as the regional editor in 1986. I founded the newspaper's graphics design desk in 1987, but quit in 1988 during a flap with management over the unfortunate purchase of a computer system. I was hired back in 1991, quitting again in 1997 — over yet another disagreement with management that had put me in an awkward position in which I felt I could not possibly do quality work.

During these hiatuses from *The Chieftain* I managed to gain experience in other areas of journalism, including freelance writing, book and magazine publishing, technical editing, marketing, and producing and managing web content. But the freelance life was difficult on many levels. There was the constant grind of trying to find assignments. At one point I actually wallpapered the small bathroom in the house with rejection notices from magazine editors. Then I learned that even once a writer was given an assignment, getting paid for it was often another challenge. Many of my memories of this time are of gloomy days when I went hopefully to the mailbox only to find the check was not in the mail.

My toils did however lead to some more lasting work arrangements, including a stint as associate editor for

Rocky Mountain Sports magazine, and then to a long-lasting relationship as a personal editor of sorts for Dr. Phil Maffetone, who had gained national recognition for coaching endurance athletes, including six-time Hawaii Ironman Triathlon champion Mark Allen. I had initially contacted Phil to interview him for a story about coaching Allen for *Inside Triathlon* magazine. We stayed in touch, and when Phil and his partner Bill Coppel decided to start a business based on his training, nutrition and health principles, I was the natural person to edit Phil's books, newsletter and website, and research health and nutrition topics. In addition to these projects, Phil had also developed a line of nutritional products and supplements, and I was involved in producing marketing materials and other content surrounding these products.

By far, working with Phil was the best job I ever had. Though the company was based in New Jersey, I was free to work from Colorado, on my own schedule. And the rate of consistent pay was the best I'd ever known. Moreover, just about everything I did for Phil helped support the healthy lifestyle that I wanted to cut out for myself. As a point of irony I "hired" *The Chieftain* to print Phil's newsletter, *The Maffetone Report*. We commonly printed 25,000-35,000 copies on the newspaper press, then trucked them to a mailing house in Colorado Springs.

This relationship lasted for several years. In 2003, Phil and Bill had decided to sell MAF BioNutritionals to a venture capital company. Other than the hard assets, Phil and I were the only two things that went with the sale. We worked together for about another year until it became apparent that the buyers' intention was to close the company down, something I never really understood. With the arrival of Harrison in 2004, I also said goodbye to the best work situation I'd ever had. And once again I returned to *The Chieftain*.

Switchbacks are bends or curves built into mountain roads and trails that increase the distance but decrease the gradient. Traveling straight up the fall line is the shortest route, but switchbacks provide a more efficient route from the bottom to the top of a big hill or mountain. In pack-burro racing cutting switchbacks to shorten the distance is not allowed. However, in this analogous race we call life, the routes and the rules are not so clear-cut.

Back in the newsroom I found a different cast of characters than those I'd worked with there in previous stints, though some were the same. I set about immediately establishing to everyone who didn't know me that I was a serious editor. I labored over each story and headline, often working 30 to 40 news and feature stories per evening. It was like riding a bicycle but it was still the same tedious work I'd done there before under the same conditions.

I was confused by how I could have possibly found myself back in that setting. I was back working at *The Chieftain* because I felt like I *had* to go back to work there.

Phil's business had been sold and my job with him was suddenly gone when the opportunity at the paper appeared. Although children had never been in my plans, I now felt the need to be some type of "provider."

So I went back. Worst was having to swallow my pride. I worked evenings and would get home often well after midnight. It seemed I'd just get to sleep at 1 or 2 a.m. and Harrison would wake up crying loudly. Then I'd get back to sleep again and he and Mary would both be up at 6:30 or 7. The waking days were hectic. The increased strain on the relationship was immediate as I resisted some of the changes fatherhood had brought to my life, and some people seemed to expect that somehow I would become a totally different person overnight. The next thing I knew it would be time to drive to Pueblo again where it was 100 degrees and the work was soul-wrenching. My life seemed like it had been turned upside down.

Also during that first year of Harrison's life I received a call from a neighbor, Jan Wilkins, who owned a small ranch about a half-mile away from my home. Their son had been managing the ranch and was now moving back to the Denver area, and she wondered if I would be interested in taking over for him. I said yes, and soon found myself feeding nine horses, caretaking two houses, and shopping for cattle.

As time passed, I managed to convince *The Chieftain* managers to allow me to work partly on a telecommuting basis. I traveled to Pueblo on Monday evenings to be the relief night city editor, then worked editing stories from home the rest of the week. On Fridays, I usually edited not only the local news for the Saturday paper, but also anything that had been written in advance for the Sunday and following Monday editions. While tolerable, the arrangement was nowhere near as interesting, satisfying or as flexible as my work with Phil had been, but I had grown to accept it for the time-being.

Until one day in 2008 when it too went away.

The word arrived like some sort of scene from a French farce and over the phone. I'd had a pretty good idea it was coming after several meetings in previous weeks in which I had been assured I was "safe." The managing editor and I had played phone tag for the better part of a day and when I finally reached him late that afternoon he seemed at a loss for words and so I broke the ice: "Steve, are you calling to lay me off?"

I've known and worked with Steve for the better part of 27 years, so I didn't feel like I was being too flip. And I had a pretty good idea what was coming. Steve explained the decision was purely financial. The newspaper had fallen upon hard times in the age of the internet and a sluggish economy. It had nothing to do with my job performance. It all came down to seniority and since I had quit so many times, I really didn't have any. I would be let go in two weeks. There was a certain irony in that the person with the world record for quitting the place being the first to get the ax. That evening after I got the news I pulled Harrison around the property on his sled. It was quiet warm for a winter evening and windless, affording a glimpse of what appeared to be a much different life.

A couple days later I decided to build a fire outside to cleanse and dispose of some bank and credit card statements and other "sensitive materials." Harrison loves campfires and he watched intently as I built a pretty big bonfire in the fire pit near the house. I had a bag of papers and also last year's well-cured Yule tree. Soon a cheery blaze was cracking. The ground was covered with snow and more fresh powder was falling. As I pulled the papers out to feed the flames, I found several blue *Pueblo Chieftain* pay stubs. There is something about an outdoor fire that tugs at the primal instinct inside all of us. Harrison was very intrigued by the flames and watched intensely, unaware of the cleansing going on in my mind.

That evening I went outside to make sure the fire was out. The storm had left, leaving the night brighter than the day with a big moon reflecting off the snow and the snow-laden branches of the surrounding pines. I looked up at the sky and wondered about my future. I decided right then to finish my final two weeks with the dignity of hard work and set an example for others who would surely be following me out the door as the newspaper cut back even more in the coming months. There is the tendency to want to be angry or embarrassed, but instead I chose to feel free.

What told me more than anything else about my many years with *The Chieftain* was my last evening of work there. A few co-workers stopped by my desk to bid adieu, tell me they were sorry to see me go. We had our daily news meeting and it was like it was just another day. In the end nobody from management came out and shook my hand, said thanks for the time or energy I'd put into the place. They were either too socially inept, too uncomfortable, or simply had never let anyone go before and didn't know how it was properly done.

That night when the shift was over I walked out the side door of the newspaper building with Stan the news editor. I wondered if perhaps Stan had been asked to escort me out of the building after putting the paper to bed. As he said goodbye he offered that he had the feeling it wasn't the last time I'd be walking out that door. But I had a different feeling. As I fastened my seat belt I looked up at the backlit sign on the side of the newspaper building: *The Pueblo Chieftain* in Old English font emblazoned on blue mountains. I started the engine and headed for home. I didn't want to think about ever going back there again.

Within the next year Mary would go back to working full-time, and I would shift my focus to managing the Wilkins' ranch part-time, picking up freelance writing, editing and graphic design jobs while also filling a stay-at-home dad role.

⁊

I took to managing Bear Bones Ranch with all the energy that I'd ever put into any job. There were nine horses to care for, two houses to caretake and several miles of fence to keep standing. Soon Jan and Ross had me shopping for cattle. The ranching job seemed to fit my lifestyle better. It was outdoors and required careful attention to detail and analytical reasoning skills, but it did not impart the kind of brain strain that editing newspaper copy had. During the period that I was doing both, it seemed like the perfect work balance for me.

I'd worked in a pet store as a teenager, and had originally wanted to be a veterinarian before being sidetracked by journalism, so this alternative career direction helped to fulfill that long-lost goal. This was a dream I shared with my high-school buddy Scott when we worked together in a pet store in the suburbs of Washington, D.C. The owner was a retired Marine Corps colonel with a crew cut who regularly pulled out a white glove to test the cleanliness of shelves and bellowed "Good night!" if the result was not to his satisfaction. By contrast, the shop's dog groomer was a gentle and kind man who commuted to the pet shop from the inner city on a motorcycle to shave poodles in the back room. He also claimed to be a pimp, though nobody believed this, and kept a big roll of cash stashed in his sock.

The Colonel sometimes had his developmentally disabled son Jeff with him. Jeff was possibly in his 20s, a big strapping guy with a crew cut identical to his ex-Marine father. Jeff was non-verbal but made some odd noises. He walked with an odd gait. He paced around the pet shop and would often tap on things vigorously with his index finger, his eyes fixed intently on the point of impact. I sometimes worried the fish might suffer concussions from him tapping on the aquariums. Jeff also had the uncanny ability to rapidly smack the back of his own neck with the back of his hand. The resulting sound was like that of someone clapping loudly. There was a young woman named Ann who worked occasionally at the pet store, bathing and grooming the new puppies when they arrived. She had confided in me that she was scared of Jeff. She always asked that I keep an eye out for her when she was working in the back room and he was around.

Once the Colonel left Jeff under our watch and, while we were busy with customers, Jeff walked out the back door of the pet store and into the back door of the neighboring gift shop. The phone rang and Scott dashed out leaving me to watch the pet shop. The gift shop was full of delicate glass and ceramic knickknacks. Visions of a bull in a China shop went through my head, and it also occurred to me that Jeff was bigger than Scott. But eventually Scott returned with Jeff in tow and no damage done.

Back then people like Jeff were merely lumped into the mentally retarded category. Only in recent years did it occur to me that Jeff was probably severely autistic. Though he was obviously disabled, could not speak, and exhibited strange and repetitive behaviors, he otherwise appeared normal. I now realize the tapping and neck slapping probably was stimming behavior. I wonder if the Colonel was bringing Jeff along with him to work to give his wife a much-needed break from watching him. Or perhaps it was out of love for his son that he wanted to bring Jeff with him into the outside world. Maybe both. I wonder if Jeff ever went to school, or if they had any place to take him for care. I wonder what ever became of Jeff.

In retrospect, perhaps the job at the pet store prepared me better than any other for the work and challenges I would encounter later in life. Over the years I'd been called into service caring for a large herd of horses when my friends Gary and Amy had needed help at neighboring Bear Basin Ranch. In fact, I'd grown quite comfortable with driving a pickup load of hay into the midst of 60 horses, shifting into four-wheel low and then, while letting the pickup drive itself, jumping out of the cab and into the bed, hacking at baling twine with a macheté and tossing flakes of alfalfa to the hungry horses. Sometimes the horses would kick the pickup or slam into the side with enough force to rock the entire vehicle. The truck's sides bore huge dents from many such incidents. The drill at Bear Bones was relatively tame in comparison, though not exactly easy work, and my memories are a blur of treading on thick ice, wrestling with frozen hoses and hydrants, dwindling hay supplies, downed fences, loose animals, and bone-numbing wind chill. Over time I'd experience the adrenaline rush of veterinary emergencies, grow good and tired of dealing with just about anything that could possibly freeze in the wintertime, form a lasting relationship with a cantankerous tractor, grow competent at managing pastures, and come to understand the many other vagaries of raising livestock in the high-altitude environment. I loved the job, and working with the animals and the land. It allowed for me to take Harrison along and for him to see the value in such work, and to actually help out. The job proved to be the longest I ever worked for anyone, and provided some of my most vivid and lasting memories.

In the beginning my knowledge of cattle was very limited, but I did know that the natural, grassfed beef business was an area of growth for small ranches. So I encouraged Jan and Ross to consider this business model, and they agreed this sounded better than a traditional stocker beef or cow-calf operation. I did a lot of research on the subject of cattle and grass, and determined Angus and Angus-cross cattle would be best suited to our operation. Also, with our altitude, buying cattle from a local rancher ensured we would get animals acclimated to the mountain environment and more likely to survive.

I knew an old rancher by the name of Virgil Lawson in Wetmore who had a herd of cattle. Over the years I'd bought a lot of hay from Virgil and had developed a strong fondness for the old guy. I visited to look over his cattle several times and he showed me what he had for sale. Ultimately I took Jan and Ross' checkbook to Wetmore and wrote the biggest check I've ever signed to Virgil for nine cows, five with calves — a total of 14 head, including delivery to our pasture. Just about everything I knew about cattle at that point was written on that check for $11,400.

The black cows arrived one spring day, stepping timidly out of the trailer and putting their heads down to the fresh grass. The weathered rancher told me he had kept them penned overnight before delivering them so they would be hungry and not hit the ground running when we turned them out. The cattle grazed calmly in their new surroundings. We watched them for some time and talked. The day was sunny and a few small puffy clouds drifted by. Finally he said with a twinge of sadness, "I suppose they look better up here than they did on my place."

I almost felt guilty for buying them.

Managing the ranch also meant caring for the herd of horses, and horses can do some crazy things. Once we were keeping a mare and a gelding separate from the rest of the herd, and since it had been dry I'd let the pair out to forage on the grass in the main compound area of the ranch. The rest of the horses were on the lower sub-irrigated pasture. I was bringing the mare and gelding in one evening when one horse named Tony came barreling across the pasture to follow them and apparently forgot all about the fence. He hit the wire like a runner at a finish-line tape, slammed into the hillside behind the fence with a resounding thud and lay still. I thought he might be dead. I started to walk over when Tony bounced back onto his feet, shook it off and galloped on up to the barn. I walked over to the point of impact and found about 15 feet of fence destroyed, wires snapped and steel fence posts bent to low angles.

I followed Tony on up the hill, where I found he was bleeding from the mouth, had superficial cuts all over his body, and had literally peeled the skin from below his left knee down the front of the cannon bone in a long triangular shape. Obviously my night was just beginning, and I went home to see which veterinarian I might reach.

When I got ahold of Kit Ryff he was just sitting down to dinner in Salida. I told Kit I didn't think Tony was in any danger of dying if he were to finish dinner, but the wound definitely needed stitches as soon as possible. He said he'd call when he was close and I could meet him at the ranch.

So about 10:45 I drove over in the dark and by the light of pickup headlights through the dust Kit surmised that I was right and decided to lay the horse down with drugs in order to sew up the wound. It took a little while for the drugs to take effect, but Tony finally went down in the corral. Kit went to work with his curved needle and sewed up one side of the wound. Then we rolled Tony over — he weighs about 1,100 pounds — so Kit could access the other side of the leg.

Kit had just started on the other side of the wound when the drugs started to wear off. There's really no describing a half-ton of half-doped, half-crazed horse flopping around in the dust inside a steel corral backlighted by headlights. He came down with his ass bashing the panels, bending one fairly severely. He landed on his water bucket, crushing it and sending a shower in all directions. Then, the worst possible thing happened. Tony flopped over and came down on the corral, somehow managing to hang a hind foot between two panels.

So now we had the wounded horse hanging upside down by a rear leg in the headlights with Kit holding Tony's head up by the lead rope to keep him from struggling. I tried to push the hind foot up and out of the panels, but there was too much weight on it. I tried unhinging the panels, but between the bent metal and the pressure of the horse bearing down I couldn't get the pins out.

Kit suggested that I take over the head, and he thought he might be able to get the foot loose. So we swapped places and I held the lead rope, twisting Tony's neck so he couldn't try to get up. The second Kit knocked the foot loose, I felt the sting of rope burning my hand. Tony was up, floundering this way and that, and I couldn't see anything in the headlights. I dropped the rope and ran across the corral. Kit, meanwhile, with his back to the headlights, had a better view of what was going on and rushed in to grab Tony by the lead.

We got the horse calmed down and Kit finished stitching the cut with Tony standing up. He bandaged the wound, gave him an IV pain medication and penicillin, and we were done.

When one of the cows was struck by lightning we needed a picture for the insurance company. Unfortunately the insurance company didn't tell us that until the cow had been dead a few days. The next thing I knew I was hiking up the mountain with a shovel, a revolver and a digital camera to get a photo. Expecting a bear, I found only a sea of maggots and the stench of rot and ammonia. Nothing with claws had eaten on the carcass or disturbed it, and I wondered if it had something to do with the fact the animal had been killed by lightning.

The insurance people wanted a photo that included the eartag to positively identify the dead cow. As luck would have it, that ear happened to be on the side of the cow contacting the ground. I pried the head up with the shovel and not only was there no eartag but there was no ear at all. Strange, thumb-sized bugs, orange and black and fuzzy, crawled out of the carcass.

I decided to take a photo anyway to show the eartag was missing. I set the shovel down and took a slow step toward my camera, which was resting on a nearby rock. The next thing I knew my feet were tangled with a chunk of wood, then they were above my head and I was suspended in the air. It was a rough landing, but luckily I avoided the carcass.

Apparently giving me an A for the effort, the insurance company paid off on the lightning-struck cow. I called Virgil to tell him about the first promise of money we'd seen since getting in the cattle business, and to give him the opportunity to chuckle at my clumsiness. We had a great laugh. And it proved to be the last time I ever spoke with the old guy. In just a few weeks I'd receive word that Virgil has passed away, succumbing to a heart attack while out working with his animals in a pasture at his ranch in Wetmore.

The vagaries of running a small cattle operation meant calves might arrive at any time during the year. One cold winter day I found a calf curled up against a Ponderosa pine, covered in ice and snow, nearly dead. It had been born two days earlier but had somehow gotten itself through a fence and away from its mother overnight as the storm had swept in. I struggled in knee-deep snow to get the calf to the barn, finally returning to the barn to get a horse blanket to use as a sled. Once inside and out of the wind, I immediately plugged in a heat lamp and put the calf underneath it.

A phone call to Kit brought the suggestion of bringing the hypothermic calf inside and putting it into a very warm bath. And so I put the calf on the floorboard of my truck, brought it home and drew a bath. Kit, meanwhile, was in the general area, and said he'd bring by some electrolyte supplement.

The calf looked like so much dead meat in the tub, and I had the odd thought that if it lived we might be eating this animal in a couple of years. Mary, amazingly, took charge, but then she is a nurse. She ran the water and tended to the calf in the tub. We used a lot of old towels and Mary's hairdryer to get him dry. Kit arrived and tube-fed the calf the warm electrolyte potion. Then we left him on the bathroom floor to dry in front of the wall heater. There was some comic relief and a mad scramble for tools when Harrison locked the calf in the bathroom, but luckily no damage resulted.

After some time we were able to get the calf on his feet. I tube-fed him again with the electrolyte liquid, and late that afternoon drove him back over to the ranch and turned him out with his mother. I held my breath wondering if the cow would take him back now that he no doubt smelled like our bathroom, but she seemed to recognize him right away. Overnight the temperature dove to minus 20. I was certain the next morning I would find the calf frozen stiff. But the cow had moved him to a south-facing hillside where he could soak up some southern sun. Over the next couple days she gradually incorporated the calf back into the herd. Against the odds, the little calf had made it.

At the cow corral, there were a couple of empty mineral tubs I'd filled with baling twine, old wire, and trash that I'd picked up around the corrals over the course of many months. One spring day I loaded this tub into my truck to take it to the dumpster back over at the main ranch. As I was dumping the tub I saw something moving and jumped back, thinking it could be a rattlesnake or a nest of mice. A closer look revealed two nearly fledged bluebirds tangled in the baling twine. I carefully untangled the little birds and put them into another empty tub. I stuffed some of the twine back into the first tub, then rushed back to the corral. I put the tub where it had been and placed the two little birds nearby. On the way back I decided to check the dumpster for more birds. Sure enough, I found a third baby bluebird, so I drove it back over to the corral. Would the parents take them back?

A few days later I saw the mom and dad bluebirds flitting about on the fence posts with insects in their beaks. I watched to see where they landed. The baby bluebirds, rescued from the dumpster, were spread out in the brush. And their parents were hard at work feeding them.

The day before the first day of 3rd grade we went shopping for school supplies in Pueblo. What could have been an easy and fun shopping excursion quickly became an epic nightmare with loud outbursts. When we first entered the office supply store Harrison noticed a display of Angry Birds USB drives, then threw a screaming fit when I said we could not buy one. When I gave him a choice of pencil boxes he wanted both and there was another loud outburst. I went down the list checking off each item while trying to keep an eye on

Harrison and what he was doing. He vanished once in the store while I was looking at something, which was frightening for a few moments until I was able to locate him. As we lined up to pay for the school supplies he grabbed candy off the shelves and I struggled to get him to put it back. At the checkout he wanted to swipe the debit card which I let him do, but then he demanded I let him sign the electronic pad and another loud disruption ensued.

When we finally arrived back at the car, which seemed like an island of safety during such trips, I sat down in the front seat with the door open and my feet still parked on the pavement. I sat that way for quite some time before gathering the energy, strength, courage or whatever combination of all those things to actually pull my legs into the car and drive on. Yeah, I'm a big tough pack-burro racer and all that, but in truth I was simply exhausted.

My friend Doug Wiley and his wife Kim run a small pasture-based organic farm called Larga Vista Ranch near Avondale, just east of Pueblo. From the time when Harrison was very small I'd taken him out to the farm to pick fresh vegetables and see where food comes from. Many of his first solid foods in fact were vegetables from Larga Vista Ranch.

To tour Larga Vista Ranch is to witness biodiversity in action. Chickens freely follow cattle through lush green pastures. Hogs range openly through fields where vegetables, forage crops and grain once grew. And vegetables and melons spring forth from the ground these animals previously roamed in this continuous circle of life. In addition to raising food organically and in a pasture-based system, Doug and Kim are pioneering the concept of biodynamic farming, which takes into consideration subtle effects such as lunar cycles and planetary alignments on the Earth's climate and weather patterns to produce even more nutritious and tastier foods.

It's all a part of a perfect plan for Doug and Kim, who also run a raw-milk dairy as part of their biodynamics-inspired farm. In addition to seasonal produce, they produce grass-fed beef, pasture-raised pork and eggs. Their operation serves up the most robust-tasting vegetables I've ever eaten, while also serving as a model for sustainability among Western small farms.

Oddly, the entire operation is based on a crop people don't even eat — grass. Animals turn grass and grain into natural fertilizer, and also enrich the soil in other ways. Cows cleave the grass with their hooves. Hogs dig up vegetable roots and turn the soil over. Chickens remove insects from manure, helping break down the waste and spreading it in the process. It all feeds the cycle of grass, from which springs a bounty of opportunity for these innovative farmers that affords them the uncommon status of earning their entire income from farming.

Doug has always allowed me to pick my own vegetables in late summer from the "garden" — six to eight acres where he and Kim grow eight to 10 varieties of sweet peppers and chiles, heirloom and cherry tomatoes, watermelons, cantaloupes, honeydews, and squash. Typically I call Doug when I see a hard frost coming on the weather report. His response is invariably, "You better get down here!"

I'm there mainly for the big sweet peppers — brilliant red and orange corno di toro, yellow corno di toro giallo, red and green cubanelles. I pick and freeze as many of these sweet peppers as I can each year, and also pick a good amount of the spicier chile peppers, which I have roasted at another nearby farm and then also freeze for use through the year. We'll also commonly bring home tomatoes, butternut squash, the odd watermelon, and sometimes a pumpkin.

I'm also there for the crisp blue sky and golden afternoon and evening light that seems to emanate from Doug's fields at that time of year. I'm at home in the mountains, but these broad vistas also speak to me during the harvest season. On one such golden evening at the farm, Harrison and I bustled through the rows of peppers looking for the best. Doug employs a field worker named José to help with the vegetable harvest this time of year. As the pressure builds to get the vegetables harvested before they go to waste, José sometimes brings his wife and two kids to the field to help out. I'm certain they are Spanish-speaking only, and since my conversational *Español* is limited we usually nod and say hello and go about our harvesting.

We were working our way through the rows of peppers when suddenly Harrison went into a bad tantrum. José and his wife looked over at us and then quickly back to their work as Harrison screamed, stomped and struck out at me. They seemed a bit perplexed by his behavior, and the kids' gazes lingered longer, I think trying to assess what was happening. I had to think, *I wonder what they think is going on? Do they have any idea? Should I try to say something?*

At these times I am thankful for wide-open spaces. The sound is diffused by the expanse, and seems to be absorbed by trees and plants and the earth itself. Wild animals and most livestock seem more accepting of it than other humans. Soon Harrison calmed down and we all went back to picking peppers in the warm and quiet evening air. Because the incident troubled me, I later looked up the word "autism" in Spanish just in case I ever needed to know it. *Autismo* is Spanish for autism. But would they understand even if I spoke it? Language, culture, autism . . . a strange combination I could only have stumbled upon in a field full of vegetables.

॰

One day when I dropped Harrison off for his piano lesson, Phyllis' husband Don pulled me aside and asked me if he could ask a favor. The answer was yes before I even knew what he wanted. The Bishops had become such an important part of my immediate community that I would do almost anything for them. Don then began to tell me the story of an old family friend who had spent 30 years developing a water diversion system that would essentially pull runoff from one high-lake drainage and send it down another watershed, where he could then use it to irrigate his fields.

Over the course of three decades this old codger had spent summers digging and blasting and constructing a wooden sluice to reroute the snowmelt. When at last he opened the gates that would send this crystal-clear water from the high country to his fields — the work of his lifetime — he was shut down by the authorities. Diverting water was illegal without the proper permits. He never realized any of the fruits from his many years of hard labor.

Decades ago as a young man, Don had been exploring the remains of the project, and found the anvil used in its construction. He laid claim to the treasure and stashed it, making note to someday return. And life goes on. Fast-forward, and Don is now in his 70s. The favor he was asking was for me to help him look for the anvil, and pack it out if we could find it. He wished for it to be placed in a local history museum as a testament to the story of his friend's toil. Of course I agreed.

So on a glorious fall day Don and I struck out on the trail with Laredo as our pack burro. There was first a long trek on the rocky and undulating Rainbow Trail just to get to the route that would take us up the drainage where the anvil assumedly awaited. The aspen and scrub oak burnished the landscape with autumn color, and dark storm clouds formed a backdrop that held the promise of a changing season. We stopped for lunch at the intersection where the trail to the lake left the Rainbow Trail.

A bitter wind and a cold drizzle began as we ate our sandwiches. I checked my pack to make sure the waterproof matches and space blanket were still in there. Then we continued on our way. Oddly this new trail was relatively flat and smooth for a short distance. But then it pitched steeply upwards. We went slower and slower. Clearly this climb was a huge challenge for Don. I would walk ahead with Laredo and wait. Sometimes Laredo would bump me with his nose as if to urge me on. Each time when Don caught up I greeted him with a smile.

He told me about walking in there with his family as a child. Then with his own wife and kids as an adult. Then we would walk on. I stopped beneath the shelter of a big spruce to wait. The drizzle turned to snow. This time when Don caught up I felt an overwhelming admiration for his determination. However, I also could see in his eyes that today we were probably not going to reach the place where he had stashed the anvil. He said, "let's go another 300 or 400 yards and then make a decision."

The snow was floating down in big flakes as I waited in a grove of golden dwarf aspens, and when he got there he said, "I'm ready to go back home."

Through the gently falling snow I could suddenly see the trails like this that lie before all of us. The trail I would be taking in the years to come. It had never been so vividly clear that time waits for no one. There would come a day when I could not do the things I can do now, could not do what I have done for decades. Some day our dreams — the treasures we spend our lives thinking about finding — will be out of reach. I could only hope that I would greet that day with the grace and dignity that Don did.

Don sat down and we talked about it. He said we were probably only a mile from the anvil. But we were a lifetime away. I wished silently we had chosen a better weather day, or had started earlier. The effort he had made to get this far was nothing short of heroic, but he could not go on. Though he'd hiked to the top of this mountain valley many times in his life, he related to me his realization that this was probably the last time he'd be on this trail. As melancholic as this seemed to me, Don seemed to be OK with it. We started back down in the quiet snow.

As we got closer and closer to the truck the sun re-emerged, and Don's spirits seemed to rise in the evening's warmth. We'd perhaps brought back something even better than an old hunk of metal. But still it calls to me. I've been back to this trail since that autumn day, looking for the anvil. Still it remains up there. It or the idea of it. This thing of which adventure and dreams are made.

᠉

Her full name was Full Tilt Boogie and I'd been beaten by her before. In 34 years of racing burros I'd never raced a jenny. Curtis and I talked it over. He was confident. I was unsure. Ultimately Mary, Harrison and I drove up to Buena Vista on a golden October day. The peaks of the Collegiate Range were crisp against the cobalt sky and some determined golden leaves still clung to a few hardy aspens. Curtis' house was much as I had remembered it from decades ago, though showing the weathering so common to mountain homes as they age. Books and films were stuffed into shelves. Papers, magazines and more books were strewn willy-nilly on the table with his familiar scribbling, highlighting and notes off to the side. Dirty dishes were stacked on the countertop and in the sink. There were no artisans hanging out, and no harmonica music in the background. His mother had passed that previous year. In fact Curtis' house seemed more lonely now than I could have ever pictured it. On the walls were hanging the framed photos and yellowed newspaper clippings from the glory days of his own pack-burro racing career.

Curtis had won three World Championships in his day. But now in his 60s his knees were shot and the snap was gone from his legs. He still ran in the races, but more for the fun of it than the competition. In recent years he had put more effort into his own breeding program for donkeys, and had developed a new focus on exhibiting donkeys at various shows in events such as "Halter Jack," "Western Pleasure," and "Single-Hitch Driving."

Curtis won his first World Championship with a wild burro named Hayduke, and then his second two with a burro named Oscar, born of wild parents in captivity. He was fascinated by the naturally selected traits of these feral animals — compact conformation, low heart-to-body-weight ratio, hard feet, determined spirit. There was also this idea that the right animal could make the sport more interesting and competitive — providing an edge for those who might not be the greatest runners or best athletes. People like himself . . . and me. This notion that a pure racing animal could be bred is a given in horse racing where millions of dollars are spent in attempts at building the perfect beast. But adopting this same approach in a sport as esoteric as pack-burro racing, where the stakes are comparatively chicken feed, was at once a Quixotic and bold undertaking. Over time, Curtis would be contacted by the Mexican government looking for stock to rebuild the country's burro herds, and by the U.S. government looking for animals to use in Middle Eastern countries. And he'd develop a line of stock sought after by pack-burro racers and other people looking for donkeys for special purposes such as packing or riding.

Curtis assembled a herd of wild jennies through the Bureau of Land Management's adoption program. These animals would provide the wild genetic component. Simultaneously he began to study the bloodlines of the American Jack Stock, which originated from those first mammoth donkeys given to George Washington. These animals were popular with breeders looking to breed mules for draft, riding and packing, and at mule and donkey shows such as Bishop Mule Days and the National Western Stock Show. Over the years he bought and experimented with several of these mammoth and large-standard breeding jacks, which brought size, longer stride and calmer temperament into the equation.

But breeding for certain characteristics in donkeys is a bit like winning at pack-burro racing itself — both are akin to catching lightning in a bottle. With millions of years of genetics on each side of the equation it's a real crap shoot in terms of what you might expect in the way of foals. Curtis' breeding program over the years produced a wealth of wonderful animals. These were large-standard and smaller mammoth donks that could race, be ridden in the backcountry and win ribbons in the show rings. One of these cross-bred donks named Wellstone won the World Championship three times with runner Bobby Lewis, and another, Kokomo, was the first jenny to win the World Championship with runner Karen Thorpe. But some of these animals had faults as well. The mammoth bloodlines added size and stride length, but could also contribute to coarse bone, big heads, mild or dull spirit. Some of these animals were not racing material but proved to be great backcountry packers and saddle donks.

Then there was Boogie. Of all the animals Curtis' program had produced, she was perhaps the Holy Grail. She was the daughter of a wild jenny named Hillary and a black mammoth jack named Massai. She was the size of a small horse and literally floated at a trot or even a fast walk. She had a refined head and bone structure, a determined spirit and natural athleticism. In this one animal Curtis' breeding program had attained the perfection he'd spent years trying to create. She had won two shorter pack-burro races at Buena Vista and Leadville, and had proven herself in riding and halter events in the show ring. And yet she had not won a World Championship. She had lifted some pack-burro racers to incredible highs and brought others to tears. Out of a hunch and in a stroke of genuine friendship and genius he had the vision that this animal could somehow help me rise above some of the cards I'd been dealt by life and find some sort of triumph in the madness.

Above all Curtis had always encouraged me to write. Despite my grievances about limited audience, incredibly poor financial reward, and fewer people reading in this digital age, he was relentless in his insistence that I write. He was impervious to my complaints about the poor compensation and relative difficulty of writing and that I didn't really enjoy or wish to continue with it. Once, he sent a check for $100 to *Colorado Central* magazine, a regional publication for which I'd written a monthly column for many years, with a note that it was to be used to support my writing. The publisher forwarded the amount to me with my next column check. That $100 was roughly twice as much as the magazine paid me per column. Whenever we talked he would ask, what I was working on, what was I *writing*? More recently he'd left a copy of Tom Groneberg's *One Good Horse* for me alongside Highway 96 near my home with the inscription "For Hal – This is 'your' book. You have one in you … and better." Groneberg's book is about a writer/ranchhand in Montana who wants to train one last good horse while coming to terms with his son's Down Syndrome. Over the years Curtis and I had shared many of life's triumphs, challenges and tragedies. In this spirit of brotherhood and friendship he was offering Boogie to me for one race. If there was any story to tell after it was over, perhaps, he was suggesting, I should write it.

We walked out to look over Curtis' burro herd in the corrals, at last arriving at a corral full of jennies and foals, including Boogie and her yearling daughter, Mary Margaret. We haltered Boogie and led her out to the nearby trails where I had my first experience with running alongside her. She led on a loose rope and she seemed to have one speed and that speed was go. There were hunters dressed in orange out in the woods and I worried one might mistake her for an elk. At one point as we crossed a dry creek bed Boogie bolted up the opposite bank and broke away from me. I didn't catch up to her until we were nearly back to Curtis' house. Then in a leap of friendship and a leap of faith we loaded Boogie in the trailer and I drove away. When we arrived back at my ranch she stepped out into the bright moonlight and floated down to the corral as if this had been her home all along.

When Harrison was only a few weeks old he met Mara, who would prove to be his closest friend, ally and advocate — in some cases his "lawyer" — for his first few years in school. While most of the kids he grew up with seemed to have an understanding and open acceptance of his differences and behaviors, Mara took it a step further, helping him through difficult situations, explaining his behaviors to other kids, always inviting him to her birthday parties, Halloween trick-or-treat outings and other functions. It helped that her parents, Monica and Mick Backsen, were among the more progressive parents in town, and Monica had been a school teacher and principal so had a deeper comprehension of Harrison's challenges. I think Mick and Monica went to great lengths to explain Harrison's autism to Mara, and so she had a better understanding for her friend than the other kids. Plus, she was clearly a step ahead, both in academics and maturity level, of the other students in her class — I would often joke that Mara could skip a few grades and just go on to college. I think because of her advanced levels of understanding she found Harrison more interesting than her other friends. Once in second grade I overheard her defending Harrison's behavior to another kid on the playground after school, explaining that Harrison had "learning differences."

Mara also had a slightly bossy component to her personality, and could be somewhat overbearing in her dealings with Harrison. Several times I had to referee disagreements between the two, and on a couple of occasions at the school playground Mara reported to me that Harrison had shoved or hit her and I would usually ask him to apologize, and then when he wouldn't I would apologize to her for him and we would leave. She was extremely patient and forgiving when most other kids would have written him off.

As time went on I could count on Mara to tell me what was going on with Harrison at school. It was like having an undercover agent in the classroom, and she would sometimes report to me about things I otherwise would never have known. She knew more about Harrison's school assignments and work than he did, and on several occasions I would call the Backsen household to ask Mara to explain the homework assignment when Harrison was unable to communicate it. Many a time she would walk out the door of the school and right up to me, beaming upwards in her big plastic-rimmed sunglasses to report the day's happenings with Harrison, tell me what Harrison's home assignment was, or what he needed to do to complete some project in class. Reliably she would tell me about something Harrison needed to bring to school in order to participate in a certain activity the next day, and if she hadn't clued me in I never would have even known. Sometimes she would relay to me something funny that Harrison had done in class, like breaking out into a song in the middle of the teacher's lecture. When Harrison turned up one day with his fingernails coated in nail polish, Mara knew exactly who painted them at recess. If other kids were picking on Harrison or taking advantage of him in any way she was quick to report it to the teachers and then let me know as well.

Mary and I, along with Mick and Monica, had concerns that Mara's overwhelming attention to Harrison's needs and safety had become too much of a self-imposed "responsibility," and we did not want it to be any sort of stress for her. But Mara seemed to enjoy being Harrison's advocate, and there really was no keeping her from the important job, as she apparently viewed it, of being Harrison's best friend.

⁊

West Texas horse trainer Buster Welch said that "every really good horse is a freak. Anybody who sets out to do something unique is going to acquire the status of a freak in his own family." I found immediately that Boogie was a freak of the best kind. She was big and strong, and ran with a big floating trot. As fall turned to winter I worked with her steadily, building a base and a bond. Although I'd seen Boogie in action and now had a working understanding of her I still was not confident she was the animal that would get me to first place at Fairplay again. She was no spring chicken herself, and she was full of surprises. Plus, she was a jenny and only one jenny had ever won in the 65-year history of the race. Still, I recognized the familiar sense of adventure in training a new animal for the race. And I really didn't have anything to lose.

Boogie was at once a conundrum of talent and mischief, size large at 14 hands and 1,000 pounds. When she moved out down the road her gait was truly impressive. However, she also had days when she really could care less about training and tried her best to get out of it. I thought I'd seen it all in three decades of training burros, but her bag of tricks was weighty, leaving me at times wondering just what I'd taken on. She caught me at unawares many times. I learned she could turn on a dime and rip the rope right out of my hands, then take off at a gallop straight up a hill, leaving me to chase her all the way back to the corral. She could also cut left in front of me at a dead run out in the open and leave me flailing at the end of the rope like a 160-pound rag doll. From a big trot she could spook at a dark spot on the road, stop in her tracks and leap backwards with all the authority of an entire NFL defensive line. Over the months she taught me to anticipate some of her antics before they even happened, and that I was still quick enough to stay a step ahead, and fit enough to steer her back on course.

As we gradually began to put in longer efforts, I thought if she didn't go psycho on race day she still had it in her to win. The bigger question remaining was, did I? One can only catch lightning in a bottle so many times. I'd done it six times with two other burros, but could I do it again at my age with a third animal? At 53 my body seemed to be responding to the training, and some of the usual foot and ankle problems were absent. Still, I was dealing with a lot of stress in my personal life, the strain of life with Harrison and the seemingly ever-present economic realities of the rural lifestyle. I knew after 20 miles the real race would be on and all bets would be off. Plus, that was about where I'd taken the tumble the year before.

Of all the holidays, Halloween is the one festivity that seems to turn out the entire Westcliffe community. If it's a school day the kids strike out as soon as the bell rings at 4 p.m., swarming in costume down Main Street, many with parents in tow, to the downtown business district. Some of the adults wear costumes as well. It amounts to a street party as the kids trick-or-treat the various shops and restaurants in the golden sunlight. For the grown-ups it's a chance to socialize, and take time to actually talk with people you often only share waves with on the highway.

Over the years, Harrison has gotten much better at the drill and the trick-or-treat routine has become less stressful. This year he had chosen to go as the "No. 2," and our neighbor Nancy Hedberg had sewn a giant costume in the shape of the numeral, complete with eyes and a mouth. Unlike other years this time he often was seen leading the way in his little group of friends' quest for candy.

It wasn't always this way. I can still remember the first years when he'd follow the other kids into the establishments, and then quite often not find his way back out. Inevitably Mary or I would have to make our way through the sea of kids to find him wandering around in the store or sidetracked by something inside. A couple of times he passed right through the store, through the back office and into the alley. Some social skills are still lacking. Rarely does Harrison greet the proprietor with a proper "trick-or-treat" or say "thank-you." We're still working on that. But at least he doesn't vanish inside the store.

It had become customary for the Backsens to host a Halloween dinner party for kids and parents.

Afterwards we take the kids out to hit up some of the neighboring homes for more candy.

Actually candy and autism are a really bad mix. It's a concession we make to allow him the social experience. After Halloween is over we toss most of the sugary GMO-laden junk. But this year Harrison definitely ate too much of the junk early. At the party there were a couple of disruptive outbursts. Afterward, when we went out in the dark for more trick-or-treating, he did what he had not done in years — at one doorstep he dashed past a woman holding a bowl of candy and disappeared inside the house. His friends crowded the doorway, and I stood on my toes trying to see what was going on inside. Finally he came rambling back out the front door.

At last another Halloween appeared to be over and we were driving home from the festivities. At the point where our road turns off the highway there was another vehicle out ahead in the oncoming lane moving very slowly. I judged its speed and distance, then went ahead and made the turn. As I drove down the county road, I noticed in my rearview that the car had turned off the highway then stopped. About a mile later I noticed it was moving. As we rounded a bend it appeared the driver was flashing the brights.

I kept on driving. But the car drew closer and the headlights were clearly blinking more frantically. Here it was, Halloween night, and I wasn't sure if it was someone needing help or whether it was some drunken crazy person, highway robber, a case of road-rage or whatever. Finally we reached a place where there's a sharp hill, a cattle guard and a driveway pullout on the right. As I passed over the cattle guard I cranked the car around in the driveway entrance, facing the driver of the following car and ready to roar away in the opposite direction if necessary.

What pulled up was an old man with Alzheimer's, disoriented and lost. He first apologized for alarming us, but beyond that the discussion was muddled at best. He was aware enough to acknowledge he was lost and wanted help, but when I turned our car back around he apparently then thought he had been talking to two different people. He was 83 years old, driving a car around on Halloween and didn't seem to have a clue where he was or how to get home.

Mary went into nurse mode with evaluative questioning while I found the miracle of cell-phone service right there and called the sheriff's office. The dispatcher seemed to know exactly who we'd found, and said his wife had reported him missing that evening. Could we wait with him until the deputies arrived?

Of course.

We tried to make conversation as we waited. He was incredibly polite. We asked about his career life, his family; despite his mental lapses he was still quite sharp about these matters. Meanwhile he seemed preoccupied about his oxygen bottles. Were they in the back seat? Yes, they're right there I told him. He asked this two more times. Once he got out and checked the bottles for himself. Then he asked me about the bottles again. It was a strange mix of memory loss and obsessive-compulsive disorder, which I have struggled with most of my life. and which I now am aware also often accompanies autism because I see it commonly as a component to Harrison's behavioral traits.

All the while Harrison sat in the back seat of our car, happily sorting through his Halloween candy. The bright but waning gibbous moon was low in the sky over the Wet Mountains and I stood outside between the cars, my son with autism in one and the old guy with Alzheimer's in the other. One in his early years and the other surely in his final few. One preoccupied with candy and the other with oxygen bottles. One with poor social skills and a near photographic memory, the other ultrapolite but unable to remember his way home. The differences were striking, but some of the parallels were unnerving.

Finally the deputies arrived. The old guy asked if he could drive his car home and one of the deputies politely told him they wanted to make sure he made it home safely. The old gent politely agreed. They helped the old guy into the passenger seat and soon he was on his way.

≈

It surprises some people to learn that writing is not easy or all that enjoyable for me, and does not come naturally. What originally drew me to the field of journalism, and subsequently writing, was actually photography. It was just that over the years I found the skills of editing and writing were more in demand, and truly I had converted my photographic mind to one of a writer. For me a picture really can paint 1,000 words. It's difficult for people to grasp that I often picture a written essay as an image or series of images before I ever write it. It forms in my head and then I project that image into words. Sometimes it's easy to get those words out, and sometimes not. This also may explain why my writing tends to be in a short rather than long form. It's my way of processing what I see around me. As Temple Grandin simply puts it: I see things in pictures.

I first became interested in photography in high school and joined the school newspaper staff. I saved to buy a Minolta SRT 101 film camera. My folks later bought me some darkroom equipment and we turned a small bathroom into a makeshift lab where I could develop black-and-white film and make prints. I continued to develop my own film late into my 20s when I edited the *Leadville Herald Democrat*, where the darkroom was literally in an old morgue and I took as many pictures as possible for each week's edition. After that my interest in photography began to fade, mainly because I was weary of the time and expense of dealing with film and developing.

Digital photography changed all that, and my interest in photography was renewed as cameras and computers improved. It also seemed fitting with my journalism career on the wane to return to the starting line. When I was let go by *The Chieftain* I went through a period in which I could not see the beauty around me, I think because I was partially blinded by the idea of a career that to a large degree had disappeared. Blinded by words and depressive thoughts, I'd become inured to the scenic beauty, natural landscape and animals that are so ever-present. I am embarrassed to admit there were times while rushing Harrison to school and contemplating my economic future I would look up at the mountains and curse their beauty. I had moved up here to escape reality, and somehow The Universe had tracked me down and brought it to me.

When I picked up a camera again it was to view the world around me in the light it deserved and to share it with others. I chose a high-quality pocket camera to replace the bulky film light box I'd previously used, following the philosophy that the best camera to take any picture with is the camera you have with you. And I began to capture the landscapes around me. It immediately was a form of therapy.

And then I discovered the joy of photographing Harrison. Capturing Harrison in pictures rather than words is to produce an image that is as pure as he is, an image that no words can paint. In photos he's not autistic. He runs free outdoors, hiking, skiing and exploring, learning to shoot a slingshot. You can't see the hour it took to actually get him outside, hear the tantrum over a pebble in his shoe or sticker in his sock. Or two miles of shrieking after a tumble on the trail. The picture is purely him. Photographing Harrison, like photographing the natural landscape around me, helped me during some difficult times to view him in the pure light of a father's love.

My child is not an honor student. But Harrison is a beautiful wonder of brilliance, talent and single-minded focus. The thing is, one can never tell where he might decide to place that focus. From early on his good looks and charms were apparent — one therapist even mused that his appearance would help him to overcome some of his deficits. He is musically inclined, with several music teachers saying he has the ability to sing at "perfect pitch." At age 9 he could play a piano while singing the words to a song, and he could also pick out tunes on the keyboard to songs he had only heard. When he heard songs on a CD or as part of a collection of music he could not only memorize the lyrics, he could also catalog each song by title and order in which it appeared. Months and even years later you could ask him the title of any numbered tune on any CD he'd heard several times and he could answer with near perfect accuracy.

When he was three and still riding in the shopping cart I was startled in a grocery when we passed the salad dressing section and I heard him clearly say "ranch dressing." He wasn't really talking yet, but had apparently read a label on a bottle and spoke it out loud.

From an early age I also realized he was cataloging road signs, business signs and billboards during our travels. Any change to these, say a sign missing or a new sign, could cause him severe distress — something was out of place. Or months later he might bring up a sign that he had seen somewhere but was no longer there, and tell you everything it said.

He can simultaneously seem completely unaware of his surroundings while noticing every individual detail in them.

Harrison is an artist and could from an early age draw better than most adults. He also can create incredibly intricate blueprints for buildings that he dreams up on his own, with attention to details few adults could ever imagine.

He can outrun and out-hike most kids his age. That is, if he wants to. Often he will take off out the front gate and only agree to turn back miles from home and after much encouragement. But then sometimes he might simply sit down and refuse to go on even a short hike. From early on he won his age group in small local running races, yet sometimes he would turn and run the opposite direction at the word "Go!" Once, in a sprint at a kids' track camp, he missed the start but soon caught the other kids and then took the lead, only to turn off the track, stop and stand screaming with his hands over his ears when the crowd cheered for him.

Harrison can very quickly figure out how to operate just about any electronic device. When he was just 6 his speech therapist handed him an iPad and he was using it fluently within minutes. We ended up buying one for him along with a number of speech and social therapy apps. Similarly, computers, iPods, phones, cameras, and other tablet devices seem to be second nature to him. Once when he was 8 years old Mary came home with her new iPhone, and he asked to see it. Within about three minutes he had made a video and taken two photos, and had emailed these to some of her patients in her contacts list. Only the fact that we do not have cell phone reception at the house, and that she had not yet connected the phone to our home WiFi system, kept those emails from being sent.

He is a master at figuring out how things work, especially anything to do with doors. For his 9th birthday he asked for a door closer. So we went to Home Depot and picked one out, then installed it on the exterior door to the utility room. Within days he had figured out how to adjust the speed and tension. He also taught himself how to take apart and replace entire door knob sets.

His handwriting is beautiful.

He can read almost anything though comprehension lags. Because of his near photographic memory, he has always been one of the best spellers in his class. Though he is fascinated by numbers and has a mathematical mind, problems involving a combination of math and language are often a complete puzzle to him.

They say it takes a village to raise a child and that could not be more true in Harrison's case. It's often struck me that if we'd lived in a bigger city his education and schooling may have turned out much differently, and not for the better. Many times I've thought how thankful I am that we were raising Harrison in a small town and small school environment where people know him and understand him to some degree. While we may have had more access to various therapies and "services" in a bigger city school system, he certainly would have been treated differently from the start, and likely shuffled off to "special ed" or the "resource room."

At Custer County School, however, the faculty was enthusiastic about keeping him in the mainstream classroom. While he was taken out of class for various therapies such as speech, physical and occupational, he remained with the same kids he'd grown up with all through the early years, with the help of his patient teachers and paraprofessional aides. Since grades K-12 were all under one roof at Custer County I quickly realized that Harrison was not just known to his immediate classmates, and was often surprised that wherever we went in town other kids seemed to know him and said "hi." It almost appeared his learning differences had conferred some sort of rock star status upon him in the community. Younger kids might call out to him as we walked past the park. And sometimes a high school kid would say, "What's up, Harrison?" as we walked down Main Street. I'd lived in relative anonymity before Harrison was in school, but it now amused me that I was known more popularly in town as "Harrison's Dad."

After graduating from the preschool, Harrison moved over to the "big school" and kindergarten, and Mrs. G. went along with him as his part-time aide to help him transition. Here Kindergarten teacher Lynn May introduced him to a more structured school experience filled with introductions to words and numbers, arts and crafts. Each day the students lined up outside the south door of the building. The elementary students would say the Pledge of Allegiance and then sing "America the Beautiful" before marching class-by-class into the doors for the day, which ended at 2 in the afternoon. Harrison never participated in the pledge or the singing, and I took a certain pride in this independent streak.

Those early days of kindergarten and elementary school remain a blur of stressful mornings trying to get Harrison ready for school, into the car, racing to the school, sometimes on slick roads, and then, the worst, getting him out of the car and to the line for his class. Sometimes we were late and I would be seen coaxing him screaming from the car, trying to get him to hurry into the line as the rest of the kids were saying the pledge, singing or even already filing into the doors. Often I would walk along with him in line as the kids filed in, watching until he disappeared inside. Then I would drive back home to get my chores done, do whatever work I had to do, and then race back to the school by day's end. He did fairly well in kindergarten with the help of Mrs. G. and his other new aide Michele Engle, who was introduced as Mrs. G. transitioned into a new role as part-time school nurse. However, one time when the aides were not there Harrison misbehaved badly in class, leaving Mrs. May no choice but to remove him to the principal's office, an experience that I believe left a profound impact on his behavior at school. Her quick and decisive action set a precedent for improved behavior in later years. He simply realized teachers could not put up with this sort of behavior in the classroom.

In 1st Grade school became even more structured with Donna Eldridge as his teacher. Harrison continued to have difficulty getting to school, perhaps even more so than in Kindergarten. After we arrived late for the start of class several times, Mrs. Eldredge met me outside her classroom door one morning and asked that I get a late pass from the office when we were not on time in the future. We ended up getting several. But he was getting good grades despite his difficulties. I remember once after a frustrating morning in which Mary had gotten very angry with him he was still whimpering as we arrived at the classroom door with his late pass. His new aide, Doreen Newcomb, led him inside to his desk and and I heard him tell her that his mommy had been angry. She kindly assured him that it was OK, that his mom was probably just frustrated, and he seemed to settle down as I walked back out the hallway, thinking how amazing it was that there were people like Doreen and all the other teachers and aides who possessed the kindness to help him get through the day.

The big class project for the year was about dinosaurs, and so we visited a couple of gift shops in Westcliffe and picked out some plastic dinosaurs, then collected some rocks and plants for a diorama made from a cardboard box. We even included some sort of flying lizard that I rigged with fishing line so that it appeared to be flying. The project may have been more fun for me than for Harrison. Later, the kids performed a skit based on the dinosaur theme. Harrison had two lines and I went to the daytime performance with all the anxiety that any stage appearance brought on. I breathed a sigh of relief as he took the microphone, stood before the audience and said his lines perfectly.

Second Grade proved to be an even bigger turning point with Leanne Stover as his teacher. For the first half of the year we continued to have problems getting to school. It had been suggested by therapists, the special education director at the school and teachers that we give the school bus a try. One therapist had told us she'd seen autistic kids make tremendous strides when they had been allowed to ride the bus and given the responsibility and sense of independence that goes along with this.

I was hesitant. Here was my son who had once disappeared out the door of the preschool and who I had to encourage into line each morning and then watch all the way to the door just to be sure he arrived inside the school. Now I was to expect that he could suddenly get out of a bus at the back of the school, find his way into line and get to the classroom on his own. Not to mention arrive there with his hat, gloves, backpack and lunchbox. The thought of this was frightening but we ultimately decided it was worth a try. I would continue to pick him up at the day's end.

For his first bus ride we talked it over with him several times. The bus stop was about a mile from the house and Mary and I both drove him there and put him onboard. Then we followed the bus all the way to the school, watched as he got out and shadowed him to the playground. We had arranged for school staff to take over from there and make sure he got into line and inside.

For the first few weeks it was nerve-wracking for me as I drove him to the bus stop every morning and then returned home to wait for the reassuring email from Leanne that he had indeed arrived in class. This new schedule added an hour of freedom to my day, saved fuel expenses, and also took away a lot of stress of coaxing Harrison from the car to the school. Since he liked to ride the bus he was more motivated to get ready on time. Whereas he never cared about getting to school on time when I was driving, he absolutely did not want to miss the bus.

One morning we arrived at the bus stop just as the bus was pulling up. Harrison freaked out a bit and took off running with his backpack then tripped on a jagged chunk of ice and went flying forward onto the dirt road. I ran to help him but he jumped up screaming and ran for the bus before I could assess the damage. That morning as soon as school was in session I got a call from Mrs. G., who was working as the school nurse. "What happened?" I told her about how he had fallen and she said, "Well, it looks awful. You're going to have to come and get him." When I arrived at the school I could see that he had apparently landed right on his face in the gravel when he fell and it was a mess of road rash. Good enough for a day out of school, and so he went along on ranch chore duties with me and we made a trip to nearby Rye to buy stock salt from my supplier there.

I always appreciated Leanne's kindness whenever issues arose surrounding Harrison's behavior. Once when I arrived to pick him up at the end of the day she motioned me aside and I wondered, what now? With a slightly uncomfortable expression she told me, "He's been trying to kiss kids on the playground." I remember responding with a pained and puzzled, "What?" I could not figure what would inspire him to try to kiss other kids. I talked to him on the way home, telling him that kissing other kids was inappropriate and asking him why he was doing that. He didn't answer but he seemed to understand the inappropriateness of it. A few days later his little friend Mara got to the bottom of the issue, discovering that another kid in the class had been putting Harrison up to this during recess, telling him to kiss another boy. Mara reported it to another teacher and kissing was never a problem again. But it was a disturbing introduction to how some people, even little kids, could take advantage of Harrison's inability to understand social construct and rules.

Likewise, another time Leanne met me at the door after school to tell me that Harrison had been spitting on other kids on the playground. Again I was miffed. Where would he have learned spitting, anyway? And why would he spit on other kids? I figured like the kissing incident it had to be from other kids on the playground, so I decided to just lay down the law on the drive home from school.

"Hey, Mrs. Stover tells me you've been spitting on kids at school."

There was silence.

I followed up on this sternly. "I want you to know that if I ever hear about you spitting on kids at school again I'm taking your iPad away for a week. Do you understand that?"

There was more silence.

"Do you understand?"

"OK," he said.

The next day when I arrived at the school Leanne reported that he had spit on a classmate just as school was letting out. I'm sure I let out a heavy sigh, and said "OK. I'll deal with it."

On the way home I told Harrison: "Mrs. Stover told me that you spit on River. So I have to take your iPad away for a week."

He screamed and howled and thrashed around in his car seat the entire 15 miles home, and when we got there I put the iPad away where he could not reach it. He soon quieted down and accepted the consequences. He never spit on anyone again.

Since the preschool graduation debacle any sort of school production, like the annual Christmas program or a class skit, was the source of great anxiety for both Mary and myself as parents, as well as for the teachers. We all wanted badly for Harrison to participate with the other kids but we could never be confident how it would turn out. We certainly didn't want Harrison's behavior to have any negative effect on the other kids' experience or their programs. A couple of the Christmas programs turned out to be complete embarrassments, and in one case Mary actually had to go up onto the stage to help him get back with the program.

Third grade with Jeanne Heinrich seemed to be a year that allowed us to all catch our breath. By now getting to school on the bus had become a familiar routine, and some of Harrison's behaviors at school had become consistently better. This was Jeanne's final year before retirement and her approach was very calm. She had a way of getting the work out of Harrison without pushing him too hard. She was always quick with the reassurance to us as parents that Harrison was "such an awesome kid." Harrison seemed to enjoy third grade so much that he typically did not want to leave after the school day was over. I would often wait for several minutes outside as he slowly gathered his belongings and made his way to the door.

Rhonda Livengood was Harrison's aide in Mrs. Henrich's class. I'd known Rhonda for years because she also worked for the post office as a part-time mail carrier. I appreciated her no-nonsense approach with Harrison's behavior and he seemed to respect her authority. She could also joke with him at the right time, and for months he would repeat her humorous attempt to get him to quit messing with the school doors with the loud announcement: "Harrison Walter, step away from the door!" In fact one day I arrived at the school to find a sidewalk chalk drawing depicting Mrs. L. shouting those very words.

For the first time in third grade we went to the Christmas program and Harrison actually participated fully in the show without incident. Other parents who had witnessed some of the previous years' debacles actually congratulated us after the program. When another father looked at me and said, "He did a good job!" I actually had tears in my eyes.

But third grade did have some moments. One snowy spring afternoon I arrived a couple minutes late to pick Harrison up from school. I never worried too much because he was almost always late getting out the door. As I drove up I saw Mrs. L. standing outside in the slowly falling big, wet flakes and Harrison messing with the door. Her hair was curling in the dampness and I could see she was upset and somewhat perplexed, perhaps near tears. I wondered what possibly could have happened to bring this tough woman to this point. As I listened I understood what she was going through because it had happened to me so many times. There had been some sort of crazy incident, she had reacted, and when it was all said and done there was only the frustration and no clear recollection of the precise sequence of events that had actually led to this moment. It's like these incidents scramble your brain. Sometimes it could take me hours or days to put it all back together, and Rhonda had had only a few minutes to process. While I felt badly for her, I found some comfort and relief that I was not the only person in Harrison's life who'd had this experience of not being able to immediately piece back together what had actually just happened.

I've seen the stress and strain that having children places on the relationships of friends and family. I've even noticed it in total strangers. There is the sudden loss of freedom. The demands on your time. The increased financial obligations — some reports say the lifetime expense of caring for a person with autism exceeds one million dollars. If having children is your relationship on too much bad coffee, having an autistic child is your relationship on the strange combination of growth hormone and hallucinogenic drugs — there will be growth but it may reveal itself in ways you could not have imagined. At the root of it all is a fear of the future, and wondering if your child ever will be self-sufficient, and what will become of him when you are no longer able to care for him. The specter of institutional care always looms. Or worse, the possibility of your child ending up out on the streets, like so many homeless people who have psychological problems. This fear is always offset by the hope, false or not, that your child will, gradually or suddenly, snap out of it at some point and ultimately become a functional adult. Otherwise it would be all too easy to cave in.

Quite often the fathers of autistic children simply do cave in. There are no reliable statistics on this but if you meet a woman with an autistic child there's a fair chance she's a single mom. It's well accepted that the divorce rate among people with autistic children is higher than the general public, but there are also other troubling disturbing aspects to parenting autistic children. Studies show depression and suicide among parents of autistic children may be higher than normal. Even more disturbing are the horrific and thankfully rare reports of parents who kill their own children, or who carry out murder-suicides.

For certain, the amount of ongoing stress that autism places on a relationship, and the individuals in it, is higher than most couples with neurotypical children will ever experience. The stress may affect each parent in different ways. Autism finds the cracks in a relationship through different avenues, from disrupting sleep and time spent together, to the chaos placed upon day-to-day activities, to the isolation that often develops when longtime friends stop calling, and when going to the grocery or a restaurant means risking a public ordeal. Animosity can arise when one person becomes the main breadwinner or when the other person puts a career on the back-burner in order to spend that time and energy managing the child. There can be a tendency to "keep score" on who has spent more time caring for the child. When problems arise, as they so often do, it's sometimes easier to cast blame on the other partner than it is to look at the situation objectively.

Respite care can be very limiting and also costly. It also feels uncomfortable to ask family and friends to watch your autistic child because you know the chaos you might be asking them to endure, even if only for a short time. Truly some couples end up divorcing and splitting parenting duties just so they can each have "half a normal life." Still others stay together, living separate social lives, often taking nights out and even vacations on their own, knowing they are most comfortable leaving their child at home with the other parent.

Some fathers don't leave home but simply "check out" in other ways, busying themselves with a job or a hobby. There have been times when I myself have realized I was using certain activities to escape reality. On occasion I've found myself happy that some unexpected ranch chore gave me an excuse to run away from home for a while. I've also sometimes wondered if pack-burro racing might be such an escape, but then it had been the perfect escape from the real world for many years before Harrison even arrived. In either case, I haven't used either of these activities to completely check out. Everyone needs regular breaks, and a healthy interest in something other than your own child helps that child to see by example the importance of seeking balance, developing his or her own interests in life, and following passions.

Conversation with Harrison while driving home from school"

"When mom and dad die I can go to the Westin Inn and climb stairs all I want to?"

"When mom and dad die? Won't you be sad?"

"No. I'll be OK."

Long pause . . .

"And then after the Westin I'll go to the hospital where grandma went and climb the stairs there all I want, too."

"Oh, OK."

"I think that makes sense, don't you?"

"Yeah, I think that makes perfectly good sense."

"Yeah, so do I."

☙

With as much driving as I do I tend to listen to music while on the road and had heard songs by the band Mumford and Sons on the radio. I liked the folkish rock sound and on a trip to a department store randomly picked up their *Babel* CD. Harrison soon liked it even more than I did, requesting Mumford and Sons to the exclusion of all other music, and screaming and proclaiming loudly whenever anything else was coming out of the speakers: "That's a BORING SONG."

There was one song in particular which I would anticipate and then hit the fast-forward button to skip when Harrison was in the vehicle. And when I copied the CD to the iPod and his iPad, I eliminated it. This song was called "Broken Crown" and the offensive lyrics contained the F-word.

Soon our CD copy was on the iPod and iPad, which meant that Harrison had cataloged them all in his brain by title and track number. And he'd memorized all the lyrics to each song. Soon he was having questions about track No. 10 and why I was skipping it and why I had deleted it from the album on the electronic devices.

When I told him that it contained grown-up language and was not appropriate for children it seemed to only make him more curious about the song, and more determined to hear it. It became an obsession of his, and a source of constant loud nagging on his part to let him listen to it. Finally Mary caved in and let him listen to it, and we explained that the F-word was not a nice word.

Mary's rationale was that he was going to hear the F-word eventually anyway, and not letting him hear the song was only building intrigue. I didn't like the idea at all, but I figured that at least perhaps if we didn't make a big deal out of it then maybe his preoccupation with the song would pass.

But no. What happened is that Harrison then fixated on this particular song for weeks. He also had questions about what the F-word means. I knew that at some point I might find myself explaining Harrison's familiarity with the lyrics to "Broken Crown" to someone, perhaps a teacher or another parent.

Meanwhile, everywhere we went it was Mumford and Sons playing. Soon not only had Harrison memorized all the lyrics. I had too. While "Broken Crown" remained Harrison's favorite song for quite some time, mine soon became "Ghosts That We Knew." Sometimes while driving I would sing this song at the top of my lungs.

☙

Over the years the many tantrums and outbursts tend to blend into one hellish blur of anxiety, discomfort , embarrassment, and anger. It can happen at any time. It can happen for any reason. There can be a rational explanation or none. That time at the store when . . . That party/wedding/funeral when . . . That trip, when . . .

I think perhaps one difference between Harrison and the rest of us is that expressing our true feelings is not an automatic reaction for us. We may have more rational reasons for wanting to throw a tantrum, but we also usually do the editing and filtering, especially in public settings, to just not flip out over whatever we are feeling at the moment. That said, there are times I wish I could feel more free to express my true feelings, and in many ways I sort of admire that Harrison really doesn't care what anybody else thinks.

There was one incident in the Big R ranch supply store in Pueblo when I was buying grain and Harrison threw a fit over waiting to sign the debit and reader, and laid down on the floor screaming when I said no. And when I went to lift him by his hands he climbed the front of the counter with his feet, suspending himself screaming in mid-air and leaving me unable to let go of him and wondering how to get both him and 100 pounds of grain out of the double doors.

One mother of all tantrums sticks firmly in my mind. We had met Mary at her mother Rosemary's apartment, where she moved not long after her husband died. Rosemary is in her 90s. We had separate cars and Mary was suffering from a migraine headache and had to run an errand before driving the hour home. We were low on groceries and so I planned to take Harrison with me to the Natural Grocers store.

When Mary left Harrison was playing on the floor of Rosemary's small living room. I chatted with Rosemary for a while, and then I told Harrison it was time to leave. He refused and protested loudly. I told him that we had to go and he continued to refuse.

Finally I turned to his grandmother and said, "Rosemary, here's what's going to happen. I'm going to pick him up and carry him out of here. He's going to fight and it's probably going to get loud."

And she said "That's fine. You go ahead and do whatever you need to do."

So I gave Harrison one more chance, telling him also what I had just told Rosemary. That if he didn't get up from the floor and go with me that I would have to carry him out.

He refused.

And so I picked him up. At that time he was probably about 50 pounds of total disagreement. He screamed and hollered and swung his arms about and kicked. And out the door we went and down the hall with him continuing to fight and scream. I held him tight and pushed the down button for the elevator. He seemed to have calmed down somewhat by the time the door opened so I set him down to get into the elevator.

He spun around and sprinted all the way back to Rosemary's apartment.

I followed him back to the apartment and we went through the entire drama again. Only this time I did not set him down until we were on the elevator and the door was closed.

He was still sobbing softly as we walked out the door and I told the receptionist that if anyone reported any noise on the 12th floor that I'd had a problem with my son.

We got into the car and I started driving toward the grocery. As I drove I could sense the tantrum rebuilding, louder and louder from the back seat. At about the time I found myself in fairly serious and high-speed traffic, Harrison came completely unglued.

A shoe sailed past my head and bounced off the windshield. Other items were flying around the cab of the car, accompanied by the echoes of screaming and yelling. Another shoe flew into the front seat and landed on the floorboard at my feet. When I finally got the car stopped at the store parking lot there were items that had been in the front passenger seat that were clear back in the hatchback compartment. And stuff from the hatchback was in the front seat.

He was still screaming when I stepped out of the car with my cell phone. Passers-by were giving me strange looks. Once again I was surprised nobody called the authorities. I reached Mary by cell phone and told her what had happened and that there was no way I could take him into the store. I could still hear the tantrum going on inside the car. Mary agreed to meet us in the parking lot.

By the time she arrived he had calmed down and appeared completely exhausted. His hair was stuck to his forehead with sweat. He wanted to go inside and promised that he could behave. We searched out his shoes and put them on his feet. And then he was the perfect angel in the store.

She had a smooth and long trot. She floated through workouts with the gracefulness of an Amish carriage horse smoothly eating up the mileage. She ran with her ears forward, her big hooves leaving satisfying and crisp outlines in the soft earth of the roads and trails. A freak of nature, a once-in-a-lifetime animal. I loved running with her. The truth is I loved even more being seen running with her. Neighbors and people I didn't even know would roll down their windows and wave, or holler or honk as they passed in their vehicles. Back at home awaited my multiple career disorder, the trials of raising an autistic son, and the inevitable relationship struggles and self-doubt. Out on the trail with Boogie I could leave all of that behind. Out there I was truly on the Hero's Journey.

ॐ

Harrison's musical skills had always been a wonder, with some teachers marveling at what seemed to be his ability to sing with perfect pitch, a mystery since he had problems with tone, volume and inflection during normal speech, and also he seems to not hear words accurately. The fact that he could play a musical instrument while singing also demonstrated impressive musical ability. The piano lessons, when he felt inclined to focus on them, seemed to be improving his musical skills.

One day I dropped Harrison off with Phyllis for his piano lesson and ran an errand in Westcliffe, returning, as I often did, for the last few minutes of the lesson. The Bishops have a big glassed-in mud room and while waiting inside I can listen to Harrison play the songs he's learning and also get an idea for how the lesson is going.

On this day it did not seem to be going that great. Phyllis was asking him to concentrate on the lesson and a certain song and he seemed distracted. I looked out the window at the mountains to the south and wondered why he sometimes cooperated and sometime did not.

She asked him to play the song for the lesson again, and he refused. I don't want to play that song!" he said.

"Well, what do you want to play then?" Phyllis asked, frustrated.

Standing out in the mud room, I thought, oh no, here we go.

"I want to play 'Broken Crown,'" he said, which is exactly what I had thought he would say.

"I don't know 'Broken Crown,'" she said.

"I want to play 'Broken Crown,'" he repeated with an emphasis on the word *crown*.

"OK," she said with a slight irritation, "go ahead, play it."

And so I stood in the mud room and listened as my 9-year-old banged out the Mumford and Sons tune on Phyllis' Baby Grand piano and sang along, leaving blank the F-word, but then it's not like most people couldn't fill in the blank by context. Afterward Phyllis walked over to the front door and opened it. Harrison was still sitting at the piano, pleased with his performance.

Phyllis looked at me with a wry smile and asked, "Is that a song you often listen to at home?"

All I could do was chuckle. "Uh, no," I said, and then explained how he had become fixated on this song.

⁂

With Harrison there is no filter or volume control for his speech, either at home or in public. This can sometimes lead to some embarrassingly funny situations.

We had stopped for groceries at Natural Grocers in Colorado Springs. It was early evening and the small store was busy with long checkout lines. As we finished with our grocery selections I realized Harrison's voice was rising above the dull sounds of the bustling shoppers and people were glancing to see why he was so loud and what he was saying. This continued as we waited in the checkout line and I noticed that the checker had apparently been either the victim of a home hair-color project gone awry or had simply done her hair in the style of Bozo as an attention-getter. Harrison continued to chatter loudly as we finally arrived at the register. He looked up at the orange-haired checker and was quiet for just a second before blurting out loudly enough for everyone in the checkout lines to hear: "IS SHE THE CLOWEN?"

I know I wasn't the only shopper in the store fighting to keep a straight face as the checker seemingly pretended she hadn't heard him and continued on with ringing up our groceries. Back at the car I finally burst into laughter. "Is she the CloWEN?" Mary cracked a smile, too. How could we not?

&

When the family dog Ted died, I thought it was a good opportunity to bring up the subject of death and to help Harrison to begin understanding the notion that nothing lives forever. In a life that is marked not so much by the years as by the lifespans of our animals, Ted the rat terrier filled an era of sorts. The little dog was a gift from my late friend Rob, and he'd been a quiet source of company for me around the place since well before Harrison was born.

Once Harrison became mobile some animosity between him and Ted become evident. I think it was partly because the dog had to vie for attention with someone new in the house, but also because he was an anxious little dog and Harrison's noises, sudden movements and quick violations of personal space made Ted even more so. He would often growl at Harrison's approach and once even snapped at him. When Ted would growl Harrison would often taunt him further, getting down in his face, flapping his hands, stomping his feet, and grunting "ewww-ewww-eeewwww."

Since Harrison was a sloppy eater and had a tendency to spill a lot of food on the floor Ted also viewed him as a great source of snacks and meals. Harrison liked to eat at the fireplace hearth and often Ted would sit there at attention and watch intently. If nobody was watching and Harrison set down a plate or a bowl of food on the hearth and walked away from it, Ted would scarf it in no time.

One day Ted had a tremendous seizure. I rushed him to the vet and he spent the night there. He came home the next day and appeared to be recovering, but then the seizures returned and I ultimately made the difficult decision to drive him back to the vet to be euthanized.

That night I was watching Harrison eat on the brick hearth and it struck me something was missing from the picture. There was no Ted there looking for opportunity.

"Hey, do you miss Ted?" I asked.

"No," he quickly answered.

"Why not?"

"I'm glad Ted died."

"What? . . . Why would you be glad Ted is gone?"

"Because I don't like Ted."

There is just no telling where an autistic child will place his emotions. It could be on a person, a place, an animal, an inanimate object or on nothing at all. One thing I'd never banked on was the notion of my child being glad his dog had died. A few evenings later on the still night of the winter solstice I pulled on my boots and waded through the new snow back over to the hillside behind the house. The moon, just past half-full, was bright with rings in the West and the Big Dipper sprawled over the northern sky.

I climbed up to the top of a big rock and opened the urn. When I tossed the ashes I'd imagined they would scatter, and so I was surprised when they held together like sand in the moonlight, with most of them landing on and near a bush at the foot of the rock. I guess that is where they were meant to be.

I walked slowly back to the house where everyone inside was sleeping and I could see the lights of the yule tree in the window. I stopped and took in the silence. It's amazing how loudly the pines on a neighboring hillside can whisper even when there is no breeze at all.

CHAPTER 3

SINCE HE WAS YOUNG Harrison has attracted a small circle of friends who seemed to accept him for who he is. Mara, of course was the center of this circle, but it also included a few other kids his age, among them Max and Alex, who are twins. Over the years it has amazed me that these kids always invite Harrison to their birthday parties, regardless of whatever incidents may have happened in the years prior. Perhaps their parents encouraged this kindness.

Max and Alex had decided to have separate parties for their ninth birthday. Max wanted his party at the bowling alley and invited just boys. And Alex would have her tea party-themed gathering for girls at home.

The bowling alley in Westcliffe is somewhat of a community center. In addition to the bowling there's a restaurant, game room, big screen TVs on the walls and tables where people can just kick back and have a beer.

About eight boys were there for the party and ready to dive into the pizzas and soft drinks when they arrived at the table. Harrison didn't like the Sprite and I gladly went and got him a cup of water. When he reached for the water he caught his sleeve on the cup of Sprite and spilled it down the front of his pants. Much screaming and hollering followed. I luckily had his backpack, which contained spare pants, in the car, so I went to fetch that and he changed in the restroom as we notified the kitchen about the spill.

Next challenge. The electronic scorecard display already had his name entered. But, usually when he bowls with Mara, she sets it up with his number name, "165." Since Mara was not there nobody knew any better and another fit erupted when he saw "Harrison" on the screen instead of 165. Max's dad Tom went to great lengths to figure out how to change it, finally getting Harrison to settle down when the number name appeared.

It was time to bowl. I was wearing the funny shoes and Harrison prefers using the kids ramp to bowl. I coached him some and the other kids also helped him. Sometimes when the ball doesn't go where he expects it to he screams and stomps. Once, my fault, I didn't realize the gate had stuck and we sent a ball down the alley crashing into it. The game was stalled as we called the maintenance guy to fix the gate and retrieve the stuck ball. One boy's mom showed up and I passed some time talking to her. All the other parents had simply dropped their kids off and left them, not an option for me.

Then it was time for cake and presents. All the kids got a little Hot Wheels car. Harrison was wandering around with the other kids and then I saw him leaning over a pool table. Tom went down there and I could see them reaching into a corner pocket. It turned out Harrison had put his car down the pocket. So we had to call the poor maintenance guy again to get the keys and take the sides off the table. Also discovered inside the pool table were several cue chalks, plastic bubbles from gum machine toys, an aspen switch about a foot long and some other small trinkets.

At last it was time to go. Harrison thanked everyone and they offered him a balloon to take home. There was a problem about which color but he finally settled for the green one. Finally, we were out the door.

Almost to the car I realized I forgot the backpack and my sunglasses. We went back inside. Somehow, the green balloon came loose from the actual string and floated to the ceiling. Once again we had to call upon the very patient maintenance guy, this time for a ladder. From the ladder, Tom was able to bat the balloon downward while I stood ready to catch it. But mostly Tom batted it along the ceiling and we chased it around the bowling alley like that for a while until Tom realized he could actually reach up and grab it. I tied the balloon firmly back to the string.

We left again and I reminded Harrison to not let go of the string. I was glad I had retied the string to the balloon because the wind was gusting. Harrison got in the car with his balloon and I walked around the other side to put his backpack in. When I opened the door the balloon shot out like some sort of wild animal that wanted badly to escape. I tried to snag it with my free hand as it rocketed past my face but away it flew. Upward and north. We sat in the car and watched quietly as it grew smaller and smaller, a speck in the sky, and finally disappeared altogether. At that moment Harrison began to scream and thrash about in his seat. He continued with this tantrum almost the entire 15 miles home.

As I was trying to tune out the screaming I was thinking about the green balloon as a metaphor for everything we had hoped for Harrison, that he would snap out of his autism at some point, grow up, live on his own, take care of himself, etc. That hope now seemed like a balloon growing distant in the sky. We'd also been living the idea that we could make the difference, that we could teach him social skills, that we could get him through school, maybe even college, and that sooner or later things would just click with him. Obviously probably nobody can make those differences. The thought of that balloon — that hope — disappearing in the sky was both freeing and heart-breaking at once.

❧

For many years, Taos, New Mexico, has been a get-away for Mary and myself. It is where we have spent short vacations and stayed overnight on trips to points farther south. At less than three hours away, I've even been known to drive there for just the day. It's a cultural hodgepodge, with art, good restaurants, nearby trails for running both on the desert west of town and in the mountains to the east. One of my favorite trails runs along the Rio Grande Gorge Rim and offers sweeping views of the Sangre de Cristo range as it plunges into New Mexico. Taos is the ancient and sacred home to the Taos Pueblo Indians, and the name itself means "place of the red willows" in the native language. Spanish colonists had established an outpost at Taos before the pilgrims landed at Plymouth Rock. Famous scout, explorer and controversial military man Kit Carson made Taos his home base for many years and he is buried there alongside his wife Josefa. Over the years Taos has become sort of a familiar home away from home, and we have developed relationships with friends who let us stay in their second homes there. However over the years since Harrison's birth it has become more difficult to make these trips. Yet, because we are familiar with Taos, it is still one of the more comfortable places for us to visit.

With spring break and my 53rd birthday coinciding we decided upon the usual Taos get-away, with Mary's sister Janet also meeting us for the vacation. For a couple of years I'd been trying to arrange an interview with Taos musician Don Conoscenti, who I'd always wanted to write about. In fact a couple of years prior we'd made tentative plans to meet up while I was visiting Taos and had missed each other during a comedy of errors. At one point during that fiasco I was driving to Don's house and actually saw him briefly in his car at a stop sign, only to realize this after I was knocking on his door and discovering nobody was home. He had run out on a quick errand involving a guitar and I'd missed him by only a few minutes. However this year he said he would be around, and that I should check him out at the open mic session he hosted at the Taos Inn with other musicians when he was in town. He suggested I interview him while he was setting up for the show, then stay for the music. I made plans for Mary and Janet to meet me over there with Harrison after the interview, and we thought we could get dinner there while taking in the music.

When I arrived I found DonCon, as he is known, scurrying about like an Ebert's squirrel hyped on the gathering March sunlight. Fresh from the challenging Taos ski slopes he bounced around the stage area with speakers, amps and wiring, setting up the sound system for the open-mic show, which attracts some of the regions' best musical entertainment. Don quickly incorporated me into the green room scene and introduced me to other musicians as I followed him around with my notepad asking questions.

I had first seen Don perform one evening at a cafe in Salida about nine years before. I was introduced to him by a friend there and bought one of his CDs, which remains a favorite. I'd wanted to interview and write about Don since seeing him play that night. His songwriting and guitar playing are mesmerizing, and the story-telling runs the nerve line from spiritual to geographical. His album *Mysterious Light* made it into one of the top-20 played by folk and acoustic DJs worldwide. And his song "Beautiful Valley," from his *Paradox of Grace* album, describes many geographical features in Southern Colorado and Northern New Mexico. He has played at the Woody Guthrie Folk Festival every year since its beginning in 1998. He also performed on the television show *Crossing Over with John Edward* after his song "The Other Side" became popular following the 9/11 terror attacks. DonCon has produced eight albums of music, all of them on his own Cogtone label. In addition to his amazing songwriting, vocal and instrumental talents, he's also a skillful studio artist.

A life-transforming mountain bike accident brought the world into greater focus for DonCon a few years ago. Without insurance and the ability to pay for traditional medical care, the healing process was on him. He says he went from living his life at 120 miles per hour every day to being flat on his back. "Dead stop," he says. "I consider it a very beautiful journey . . . I'd do it again. It was a very cool time in my life." He said he was on his back for a month before he was able to begin walking in a pool, then with crutches, gradually working his way to walking up stairs. Today he is back on his mountain bike and pushing the envelope on double-black-diamond ski slopes, which he sees as a metaphor for what he wants to do with music.

He went back to telling stories through his music, much of it written against the backdrop of Southern Colorado and Northern New Mexico. "I write about the larger perspectives, the vistas, and the more spiritual things that are not obvious to people," he says.

"Spirit rules here," he says. "That's how I live."

At 57, DonCon told me he was starting over. "I've got to step up my game," he said. "It's on me. I'm always trying to make it better." What the former Atlanta rocker meant by that is pushing new terrain with his guitar in studio sessions with musicians like Ellis Paul and Bill Dillon. Which is really saying something — here's a guy about whom a reviewer once said: "It's sometimes hard to believe that there is only one guitarist creating all of that sound."

As my interview with DonCon ended and the music was starting up, Mary, Janet and Harrison arrived. I could see from the Green Room that Harrison was already opening and closing the front door to the inn. I could tell right away by the look on Mary's face that she could not deal with Harrison in that busy environment.

We asked about getting a table in the restaurant and were told it would be a long wait. We decided to eat elsewhere and come back.

We walked down the street to the Gorge Grill, where we were able to get seated fairly quickly but found we had the same issue with Harrison and the doors until the food came. He ran back and forth from the table to the front doors, opening and closing them until one of us went to bring him back to the table. Finally the food arrived and we were able to keep him seated for the meal. Another group arrived and took over a big table near us.

Since it was my birthday and Janet's was the following day we ordered dessert to conclude the meal, and Harrison sang Happy Birthday to us when they brought it to the table. When he was finished singing the people at the neighboring table erupted in applause. At this, Harrison totally freaked out, screaming and yelling and crying hard. Janet finally took him away from the table and back to the doors to calm him down. Mary started to explain to the people about Harrison's autism and then broke down in tears. Janet finally came back with him and we ate the Key Lime pie quietly and left.

As we walked back to the inn both Janet and Mary said they were too worn out to listen to the music. Ultimately they went back to the condo and I went back to the inn alone. There I found that Max Gomez had unexpectedly showed up and was going to play a couple songs with Don Con. I had no idea who Max was but one of the musicians in the Green Room filled me in. Max was a Taos musician who'd found some recent popular success, and had just filmed a video directed by Kiefer Sutherland based on his song "Run from You." He and Don Con were going to perform this tune.

I lucked into a small table right in front of the stage and settled in for the show. As Don and Max took to the stage, one of the open mic musicians asked if she could have a seat at the little table. Of course I said sure. We sat listening to the music and I thought how bizarre that I was sitting at a table in the Taos Inn on my birthday listening to music with someone I didn't know at all. Max and Don's performance of "Run from You" was beyond amazing, and on my walk back to the condo I thought how fortunate I was to have been there to experience it, and how far all of this seemed from my own reality.

The next day as we were driving around and listening to KTAOS Solar Radio we heard an on-air announcement that Mumford and Sons would be playing in concert at the Kit Carson Park in Taos that June. Both Mary and I turned and looked at each other. *Mumford and Sons is playing here in Taos?* Because space in the park was limited, tickets to the show would be sold only through an online drawing. Harrison immediately tuned in to the announcement. He wanted to see Mumford and Sons and asked over and over. We explained that it was by lottery only, that we'd have to enter the drawing and be selected, and that the chances were slim. He began to obsess and persisted until we finally agreed to enter the drawing when we got back home and see what happened.

～

My neighbors at Bear Basin had pastured a couple of burros on their ranch while their owners, who had sold their nearby property, searched for a new home for the critters. They were a father and son pair of paint burros. One day Boogie and I were running through the ranch on one of the roads when these burros spotted us and gave chase. Boogie picked up her trot a bit but did not get too excited about being followed by these other burros. Soon the older donkey gave up the chase, but the younger gelding continued along, following closely and sniffing Boogie's rear-end. Boogie continued on at her quick trot, then suddenly picked up both rear feet and slammed the paint burro square in the chest.

The force of the impact not only stopped the burro in his tracks, it actually blasted him backward and simultaneously spun him sideways. I was astounded by the quickness and force with which she had kicked, and brought Boogie to a stop so I could check to see if the burro appeared badly hurt. He stood there quietly in the road, apparently in shock. After a couple minutes he wandered across the road and off to the opposite side. Soon he was picking at the grass and I decided that he was OK. Still, I was impressed with how swiftly and forcefully Boogie had let fly with her hooves and powerful hindquarters. The impact could have badly injured a person. Developing a bond with a burro that serves one well when under stress in a race situation means knowing what they might do in any given situation. This serious kick was a real eye-opener, and I made a mental note to be aware if I ever found myself in such a situation again, especially during the crowded and frantic early miles of a race.

Over the years I often would take Harrison over to the ranch with me. Sometimes I just liked to take him along to see how I did the chores, cared for the animals, and to show him the sense of purpose and responsibility. Other times it was by necessity when I had to get chores done and Mary was away. I always liked the idea of a job that allowed for me to bring him along.

I had the vet scheduled to give the horses their spring vaccinations. We went over to the ranch ahead of time so I could round up the horses. It's easier if you do this before the guy with the kit full of needles arrives. Harrison liked to play in the loft of the barn so he went inside and up the stairs as I gathered ropes and halters and went out to catch horses.

There was a neighbor cutting firewood on the adjoining property and the horses were acting slightly on-alert over the chainsaw noise. One of them, Fooler, was acting especially goofy so I decided to catch him first. I walked right up to him and put the rope around his neck to hold him still while I got the halter over his nose. Fooler is enormous and I reached high to get the halter strap behind his ears. I was leading him back to the barn and realized the sound of Harrison running on the loft floor was spooking Fooler even more. In addition to being a very large horse, Fooler has a tendency to be a bit pushy. As I walked the horse I called out to Harrison to stop running because it was scaring the horses.

All was silent for a few seconds until Harrison came bursting out the ground level door, screaming and swinging his hat wildly by the chinstrap. He was angry that I'd told him to stop running. Of course this was all Fooler needed to come completely unglued. As I tried to hold the horse steady, Harrison got enough speed on the spinning hat to throw it into the air. I knew I was in trouble and decided to just do my best to drop the rope and get out of Fooler's way. I got knocked sideways by the spooked horse in the process. Sometimes the jolt from a quick reaction like this results in more damage than the actual impact. I got Harrison calmed down and tried to explain what a dangerous situation he had created for his dad. For several days I had a sore shoulder and knee to go along with my bruised psyche. But I knew I'd been lucky — it could have been much worse.

છ

If you're going to wait for perfect training weather around here you're not going to get in very good shape. At this altitude Mother Nature's "bi-polar" spring flings can bring blue skies and warmth one day and gale-force winds or heavy snow the next. Trying to make training plans mesh with the swings in the weather as well as your work life and parenting responsibilities makes getting out for longer efforts even more complicated. Basically I make plans for my longer workouts and if the weather is not absolutely absurd — like 70 mph winds or a foot of snow — I just go.

It was a damp and foggy spring day. I had in mind an out-and-back type run with a steep 3-mile loop at its far end in the nearby national forest. I'd had Boogie out over most of this course, including the first mile up and down either side of the loop. Only about a mile in the middle of this loop was unfamiliar territory to her. We left the house at a good clip. The dirt along the roadside was damp and the air seemed washed with the spring moisture. The fog hung low to the hillsides, and here and there a skiff of snow lay on the ground. Periodically we'd run into a flurry or a brief sprinkle of cold rain.

The bottom part of this loop is about 4.5 miles from home. From there the trail follows a deserted logging road up a very steep and rocky hill. Boogie had run up there several times in training. After we topped out on this hill she expected to turn around, and so I had some difficulty convincing her to make a lefthand turn and keep going. For the next mile she stopped in her tracks several times. She turned off. She spun all the way around and tried to go back. Each time I collected her and we continued on our way.

When we reached the point on the loop where she had been before I figured she would become more agreeable, recognizing where she was and that she was on her way back home. Plus, it was downhill. But no. All the way downhill Boogie continued to spin around, once yanking the rope so hard it jolted my shoulder, before spinning full circle and taking off back up the hill with me in tow. It would take me some distance at a sprint to get her stopped and turned back around.

Every burro I've ever trained has seemed to have a built-in GPS system. They know where they are in relation to home and other animals in their herd. They also seem to have a photographic memory of every trail or road they've traveled, and even every landmark rock or bush along every route. So Boogie's behavior was truly perplexing to me. This was a burro who had always blazed her way back home. How could she not know where she was? How could she not realize we were on the way home?

And the behavior did not stop even after we'd gotten down off the mountain and were on the main county road where we had regularly trained for months. About a half-mile from home she suddenly spun around again, ripping the rope from my hands. Luckily, I'd just put her through a gate at a cattle guard or she may have gone back and rerun the entire 12 miles. I had no idea what she was thinking. Perhaps the weather had clouded her brain, or the fog had confused her usual landmarks. I'd never seen a burro behave like this. I even wondered briefly if perhaps she'd gotten into locoweed.

I was chilled and soaked to the skin, and tired from Boogie's relentless efforts at making U-turns. My shoulder ached from trying to control her sudden turns. After I put her back in the corral I went inside to warm up with a hot shower, and I thought: "I'm running the Fairplay course with this burro? What if it's a cold and foggy day? What if she tries to turn around like that the entire 29 miles? I briefly considered going back to Laredo for the race. With the longer training runs still ahead I still had time to make that change if I made the decision now. But as the hot water warmed my bones I thought maybe I was already in way too deep with Boogie. I would have to see it through.

Shortly after arriving home from Spring Break in Taos, I went online and entered the drawing for the Mumford and Sons ticket sale. It was not difficult to remember to do so because Harrison asked me about once every hour if I'd entered the drawing yet. I explained to him that there was a real good chance we would not be drawn, so not to get too attached to the idea of going to the concert. When I really thought about it, Kit Carson Park was not very big. I thought the number of tickets would be very limited.

Once I'd entered the lottery, Harrison began asking each day when I picked him up from school if I'd heard anything. "Have we been selected to Mumford and Sons?" And then once or twice while driving home he'd ask again. "Hey, are we selected for Mumford and Sons?" I would patiently answer each time that I'd not heard yet.

Then one evening while making dinner, I got the email inviting me to the online ticket sale. The deadline was the next afternoon so I thought, cool, I'll just go online and buy the tickets the next morning. And I made the announcement to Harrison that we'd been "selected."

Harrison was ecstatic. "We've been selected! We're going to Mumford and Sons!" he cheered.

What I hadn't read was the rest of the email saying the tickets were limited and first-come, first-served. In other words they'd selected more people for the drawing than there were tickets. I was under the impression they'd only drawn as many people as they had tickets.

The next morning after Harrison went to school I went online to buy the tickets and found there were none left. It was sold out. I thought there must have been some mistake. I called Ticketmaster and tried to explain. No go. I'd totally missed the opportunity and had nobody to blame but myself.

When I picked Harrison up from school that day the first thing he asked was "We've been selected for Mumford and Sons, right?"

"Right," I said. I could not begin to even think about trying to explain to him how we'd been selected but that I'd missed the window. It was all my fault for not reading the entire email. I thought perhaps I could find some other way to get tickets.

The next day I went online and found that scalpers had bought a lot of the tickets and were selling them over the Internet for outrageous prices. I wrote to connections in Taos to see if they had any idea how I might get tickets and nobody did. I considered that at worst case I could buy just two tickets from scalpers and either Mary or I could take Harrison to the concert. But still, the prospect of buying even two scalped tickets was very expensive. For weeks I endured the daily questions from Harrison about the concert. I didn't know how to explain it to him. I was hoping he'd just forget about it. But he didn't.

Weeks went by and his questioning about the concert lessened somewhat but he was still asking about it daily. Then one morning I got an email saying that a *very limited* number of tickets had become available for the Mumford and Sons show. I simultaneously clicked on the link and pulled my credit card out of my wallet. The site had a little time clock running in the bottom corner, allowing one only so much time to fill out the form. I copied the code from the email and pasted it into the application, followed the entire process of typing in my information, typed in my credit card number . . . and then the site bumped me out and gave me an error message.

I tried again. And again. And again. I lost count of how many times I typed in my information. Each time the little time clock was running and each time I was unsuccessful. I kept on trying.

And then suddenly with the time clock showing only 18 seconds left on this attempt, my purchase for three tickets went through. I received an email confirming my order. This time we really were selected. The tickets would be arriving in the mail within 10 to 14 days. We really were going to Mumford and Sons.

~

Since I'd never run with Boogie in a race situation it seemed like a good idea to enter a shorter race before the World Championship. In Colorado there are as many as six shorter pack-burro races in addition to the 29-mile contest at Fairplay. One of these shorter runs is a 9-mile race in Georgetown, which is located along Interstate 70 between Denver and the major ski resorts of Summit County and Vail. The race at Georgetown is typically held on the Saturday during Memorial Day weekend, so it's a nice time of the year to get out for a first race.

While many may think a shorter race would be less difficult, this is not necessarily the case. Part of the reason for this is the pace of the shorter races is much faster. In addition, the shorter races attract more entrants, many of them beginners, which brings more unpredictability to the chaotic starts and to interactions with other competitors and their burros out on the trail. There's also very little margin for error in a short race — one small equipment failure or miscue with your animal can mean the difference between first place and 10th place. Mainly I wanted to see how Boogie reacted to a frantic start, and also to see how well she would perform under the intense pressure that a short course provides.

We had decided in previous years that taking Harrison to a burro race made for a long day for Mary, and that it was just easier for her to stay at home with him. This was sort of sad for me because burro racing was something that Mary and I had shared before Harrison was born, and also because it was something that I wanted to share with Harrison. At the same time, going to races alone allowed a brief sense of the freedom I'd known when I'd first started out in the sport decades ago. That morning of the Georgetown race as I was packing up it seemed strange to be driving off alone. As I was heading out the door, Mary told Harrison, "Say goodbye to daddy."

He answered in his loud and shrill morning voice: "My dad is going to die?"

We both looked at each other. Because of Harrison's language difficulties I'd always wondered if he even hears things the same way we do, or if his brain sometimes doesn't process sounds or speech accurately.

"I hope not," I joked.

"No, your dad is not going to die. Tell him good-BYE." she repeated.

I drove away with a slight sense of foreboding that such a miscommunication can bring about. It was a long drive to Georgetown, first down the curvy Hardscrabble Canyon, then striking out for Colorado Springs, I-25 to south Denver, 470 to I-70, then the long uphill grind to Georgetown, where I found 40 other entrants and their burros getting ready for the start. George was not there but his burro Jack was, and in the hands of another very capable runner.

Georgetown was founded in 1849 during the Pikes Peak Gold rush but it was established as a silver camp rather than a gold camp. At 8,530 feet elevation, the historic downtown area features tallish 19th Century storefronts, and narrow streets and sidewalks. The starting line sends racers slightly downhill for a couple of blocks before taking a sharp righthand turn then running along a paved avenue, passing beneath Interstate 70 through an underpass and then catching a dirt road that leads to a narrow trail.

I was slightly nervous for the start with so many inexperienced runners packed onto the narrow street, plus not really having any idea of how Boogie would react to a crowded start. I stayed in front of her until the righthand turn, then sensing that she was not overly excited by the start I turned her loose in front of me. In this way I was able to drive her around the slower runners who were ahead, winding our way around single teams and groups, at last passing under I-70 and out onto the rocky course. By this point we were with the leaders.

We could have easily left everyone behind there, but every time I tried to drive Boogie out into first place and take a lead she would spin off and carry me off the trail. She didn't want to take the lead. Finally, as the trail grew steeper, I decided not to waste any more energy on trying to break away. Besides, this part of the trail was dangerous. A look off the righthand side revealed steep dropoffs, with vehicles on I-70 looking like little Matchbox cars directly below. A misstep by human or beast could mean certain death. When the narrow trail topped out on a pass two thousand feet above Georgetown, we were following a group of other racers and I began to push the pace on the downhill stretch toward the turn-around in the small town of Empire.

There was a commotion from behind and I turned to see another burro zoom past me with the runner hanging on to the end of the lead rope and his legs turning over like a cartoon character running out of control. At last he could hold on no more and let go of the rope. The runners who were ahead of me heard the commotion and stopped to catch the loose burro, and I arrived where they stood along with the runner who had lost his animal.

Boogie could care less about all of drama and trotted right by all of them, taking the lead for a brief while. We arrived in Empire slightly ahead, but then Boogie began to spook, stopping and carrying me off onto lawns a couple of times. By the time we turned around we were several places behind again, and I just hoped Boogie would be willing to step out and take the lead on the return trip.

She did, and when we once again topped out on the little pass where the steep and narrow trail dropped back into Georgetown we had a decent lead. But Boogie would not let me lead her quickly down the trail. She was pulling back on the rope. I feared driving her ahead because the trail was so steep I might lose control of her. And so we picked along the best as we could, and by the time we reached the bottom there were two other teams right on our tail. I led her through the shadow of the underpass, and then onto a street lined with houses. The other two competitors were right behind us, driving their burros and pushing us along too. They were working together with their burros paired up and I felt like my best chance to win was to get a better lead on them and avoid what surely would be their last-second drive to pass us. I just wanted to break away from them.

On a slight uphill less than a half-mile from the finish, I pulled to Boogie's left side and then drove her ahead. She leaped out to a bigger lead for a short distance and then suddenly dived off to the right and into a yard. The two teams passed as I struggled to regain control and get Boogie back on course. Within a few seconds I had caught back up to them but now getting around two burros running side-by-side on the narrow street would not be easy. With not much distance left in the race I decided to take a chance and drove her ahead again. She took the lead, and then just perfectly drilled the two righthand turns that led to the finish opening up a narrow gap between the other burros. As I drove her toward the white line I was on the lefthand side of the street and the other two teams were just a few seconds back in the righthand lane. Tourists and spectators lined the street and were cheering. That's when I saw the car that had somehow gotten onto the street and was stopped in the lefthand lane right at the finish line. In a split second I had the presence of mind to sprint ahead of Boogie, then lead her at an angle back to the righthand side of the road, of course losing ground to the two burros behind me in the process. I just hoped she would not hit the brakes in the process. In a flash I made this move and led her across the finish on a loose rope just a few seconds ahead of the other teams.

I had not won a race in five years. Now suddenly it was clear I still had it in me and so did Boogie. While I was thrilled with the win and had gained some race experience with Boogie, her antics out on the course still made her a wildcard in my mind. I would not have another chance to test her in a race before the World Championship. On this day I had been on my game and on my toes, but I would have to be on my game for more than three times the distance at much higher altitude to win the Fairplay race. Perhaps more intriguing to me than our first-place finish was the burro Jack's 4th-place finish, more than 3 minutes behind us. I tried to find some confidence in all of this as I drove back home, but in the final analysis the only thing I could take away from Georgetown was the fact that I was still capable of winning a race and Boogie was, too. All I could do was continue my training, and then deal with whatever challenges were thrown at us on race day.

We arrived in Taos for the Mumford and Sons concert mid-afternoon and unpacked at the condo just a couple of blocks from Kit Carson Park where the show would be that evening. As we arrived we realized the main street through town, Paseo del Pueblo Norté, had been rerouted, and some locals had already set up stands selling everything from food items and bottled water to parking spaces. The town of Taos was expecting its population to triple for the show in just a few hours, and yet everything seemed rather calm.

I immediately walked the short distance from the condo over to the park to see what the line was like, and found one of the side streets was also blocked off to accommodate vendors selling goods and food. The entire town had taken on the air of a street fair, and yet it seemed not all that crowded. The show was general admission with those first in line getting the closest views. We had brought along folding chairs but they were not allowed into the park. I found the entire park walled off, and the line to get inside was already forming, but was perhaps not even a half-block long. These few people were waiting a long time to get front-rows seats. I knew we would have to carefully ration Harrison's attention span and patience. We wanted a good seat, but we also could not expect him to stand in line for hours. I also wondered with his sensory issues just how close we should get to the stage, and how much other stimulation from the show and the crowd would affect him.

One thing was for sure — we needed to eat before getting in line so when I returned I suggested we go to dinner early then get back. There is no way to describe Harrison's level of excitement. We went to dinner at Orlando's, where we commonly go for New Mexican food, and surprisingly found the popular restaurant to not be overly crowded. Harrison was well-behaved throughout the meal and eagerly ate his food without incident.

By the time we got back to the condo, got ready for the show and walked to the park, we found the line had grown considerably. The Main Street had filled with walkers and revelers, and we walked through the crowd searching for the end of the line. The line now reached south along Paseo del Pueblo Norté and then turned east on Kit Carson Road. We found the end of the line just past the Kit Carson Home and took our place with the other concert-goers on the old Western boardwalk. This landmark was actually where Kit Carson had lived back in the 1800s and is now maintained and operated as a museum. There was a couple about our age in front of us and we learned they had driven all the way from El Paso, Texas, for the show. Soon we were joined by a group of young men and women from Albuquerque behind us. As we waited we exchanged pleasantries, and also explained Harrison's autism and fascination with Mumford and Sons as he began to ask the usual odd questions and make out-of-context statements. Also, we were having difficulty keeping him from wandering from our place in the line and several times one of us had to chase after him as he worked his way forward or backward on the crowded boardwalk, or onto the street, which had now filled with people walking east to find their own places at the end of the steadily growing line.

For a short moment the line moved forward and we found ourselves under the sidewalk roof directly in front of the Kit Carson Home and Museum. This was extremely fortunate as that was about when we first heard the rumble of thunder. Soon an intense cloudburst was soaking the entire area, and water was running down the gutter. I looked around the corner of the eave to see lightning over Kit Carson Park just to the north. An enterprising fellow walked along the line selling plastic garbage bags to be used as makeshift rain ponchos. Finally the storm brandished its rainbows and as water continued to run in the gutter for some while the clouds gave way to golden sunshine. Mary set off in search of coffee, and I held our place in line. She came back with coffee and hot chocolate for Harrison.

And then the line finally began to move. Very slowly at first, with a few stops until we rounded the corner. Then the pace became more steady as we passed the Taos Inn where I'd heard DonCon and Max Gomez several weeks before. The pace picked up as we passed the gate into the park and then suddenly the line was moving very quickly as men and women were divided into separate lines for pat-down searches, and backpacks were checked for contraband. The next thing I knew we were back together on the park lawn and searching for a place to watch the show, finally choosing a spot against a tall chain-link fence that separated the main section in front of the stage with another section that was reserved for beer sales. There was a short distance between this fence and another, apparently designed to keep people from passing beers over the fence to minors and also to allow access for emergency personnel. For us, this fence limited the direction that Harrison could possibly wander off. We were both on full alert as we knew that in a split second Harrison could vanish in this crowd. The rain had provided a softness to the air and the park seemed like a wondrous place though there were several thousand people still waiting to get in and we had some more waiting to do.

For some reason it had not occurred to me that Mumford and Sons would have a warmup act before their show. Much less two warmup acts. But we watched as English performer Michael Kiwanuka and then the indie rock band Mystery Jets took to the stage. After each act there was a stage tear-down and setup that amounted to more waiting. The setup for Mumford took even longer and there seemed to be an elaborate transformation happening up on the stage.

The sun set, and it was growing dark outside when at last the lights dimmed and the band we'd come to see appeared mysteriously onstage to the quiet opening background music and guitar strums of "Lover's Eyes," followed by the low lyrics of Marcus Mumford. The song built slowly in intensity, *Let me die where I lie beneath the curse of my lover's eyes* finally reaching a crescendo at which the band released a laser light show and clouds of dry ice smoke while cranking up the volume. In addition to the main band, there was a small string orchestra and a brass band accompanying on small stages to the left and right. I looked over to see Harrison's reaction to all this and I could only see his big smile.

I had not attended a big rock show since my early 20s, and had not expected this to be one either, so the loud volume and bright lights actually took some adjustment. Also, I felt a bit claustrophobic from the tightly packed crowd. Still, the music was so phenomenal that it overwhelmed my own sensory issues. I wondered if the band might rock Kit Carson right out of his grave just a little more than a stone's throw away. Mary alternated holding Harrison up to see with holding him and dancing. A couple sitting near us had two small children that danced and tried to catch glimpses of the band through the standing crowd. I alternated standing and trying to see the show between the other spectators with sitting on the top of the chain link fence, which afforded a pretty good view but I knew it was leaving sharp imprints on my skin through my jeans. Harrison seemed to be a bit glassy-eyed, and I wondered if it was the effect of the small amount of second-hand marijuana smoke that had drifted by or whether he was actually star-struck. Medical personnel made their way through the crowd with a woman on a stretcher, no doubt the victim of over-consuming certain substances. Harrison asked why they were carrying her away and we told him she wasn't feeling well, not exactly a lie.

The band worked their way through all their favorites and Harrison sang along with each song from the *Babel* CD. Then, near the end of the playlist, they welcomed Robert Mirabal onstage. Robert is a Taos Pueblo Indian, known well for his flute music and the winner of two Grammy awards. As the sounds of his flute opened for "Awake My Soul" a chill came over my body and I was taken back to a time when such flute music may have echoed off the walls of the nearby Taos Pueblo just to the east and the canyon walls of the Rio Grande Gorge to the west. At this moment I was so totally tuned into Mirabal and the crowd's reaction that I had actually tuned out Mumford, though the lyrics to the song carried a spiritual message:

In these bodies we will live
In these bodies we will die
Where you invest your love
You invest your life.

To see Mirabal, the local, playing his music on his home turf before such a crowd was beyond moving, the highlight of the evening, but then a few moments later when the band launched into their trademark "I Will Wait" Mirabal returned to the stage, smoothly flying around the band members in a traditional Pueblo dance, joining them at the microphones on vocals, and thoroughly pumping the crowd into a frenzy. I was so stunned by this performance I later couldn't recall which songs Mirabal had accompanied. All I could remember was his flute and his dance.

The concert ended with "Dust Bowl Dance." I could tell Mary was exhausted from lifting and holding Harrison and he was tired from all the music and overstimulation too. The crowd roared and Mumford returned to the stage, opting, I thought oddly, for an acoustic performance of Bruce Springsteen's "I'm on Fire." As the band returned for a second encore with "Winter Winds," we began making our way out of Kit Carson Park, wanting to get ahead of the stampede of

11,000 people exiting at once. Within a few moments we were back at the condo, and I listened from the balcony as the band finished out the show for real with a performance of "The Cave." We were all exhausted and fell into our beds as the masses outside on the streets shuffled to their cars and rooms. I felt as if we had just given Harrison an experience that none of us would ever forget.

~

Over the years we have endeavored to provide as much early intervention and therapy as our budget and schedules would allow. The therapies are expensive and not covered by our insurance policy. Plus, there are other expenses involving travel and lost work time associated with therapy. It was through Mary's diligence and relentless patience in filling out forms that Harrison received these therapies and she also found and applied for financial assistance to help pay for them. In the early days when Harrison was identified as having learning delays, he received in-home therapies through local governmental agencies. Later, when his speech delays and problems became evident we received a scholarship from Scottish Rite Foundation that paid for speech therapy at The Children's Hospital Colorado Therapy Care in Pueblo. It was through this speech therapy that Harrison's "darting" behaviors began to subside. We will always be grateful to the Shriners for providing the assistance for this opportunity we otherwise would have been unable to afford.

Also early on we'd enrolled Harrison in a summer session at Soaring Eagles, a program based in Pueblo West that works with autistic kids. Soaring Eagles proved to be a mixed bag that summer when he was 4. We noticed that Harrison picked up some behaviors and noises from other children who were probably more severely affected. However, the summer at Soaring Eagles proved to be when Harrison finally became toilet trained, though he still had occasional accidents after that. Also at Soaring Eagles we met a young woman, Ally Garcia, who was working toward advanced degrees in therapies for autistic children. We were fortunate to be able to hire Ally independently the following summer to work with Harrison in our home.

The following summer we also enrolled Harrison in a summer program called Adams Camp that is held annually in Colorado at Snow Mountain Ranch of the Rockies near Winter Park. The camp provided five days of activities with other autistic kids, and one-on-one sessions with a variety of therapists, ranging from art and music to speech and physical. The kids were divided into groups of five of similar age. In Harrison's group only he and one other kid could speak at all. During the day Mary and I were able to run and relax a little, and I also found time to revisit some of the places I'd known when I'd worked on the trail crew at Devil's Thumb Ranch. So much has changed in that area over the years, just as so much had changed with me. We received a partial scholarship to Adams Camp but it still was a fairly expensive proposition once we had included food and lodging. We left with Harrison having had a great time while learning to eat oranges and strawberries which he previously would not eat due to texture issues. Adams Camp also marked a turning point when he began to refer to himself in the first person rather than in the second person.

The following summer Harrison received yet another scholarship, this one to Extreme Sports Camp in Glenwood Springs. Here he was introduced to a variety of summertime outdoor activities, including river rafting, rock climbing and wake boarding. Once again we were able to get a break while Harrison was at camp for the day. While there were no major breakthroughs from this experience, he seemed to enjoy the camp and the time away from his routine back at home.

Now in his ninth summer we had enrolled Harrison at Soaring Eagles once again. His fixation on doors had become all-consuming, and Mary thought some behavior therapy might help with the situation. I was hesitant about Soaring Eagles not only because of the expense and travel, but also I remembered his picking up other behaviors the first summer he'd attended. The routine became at once a stress, with a morning start time and a 62-mile commute to get there, the program running four days a week. It was also a lesson in seeing what other parents were going through, as they arrived with children from all reaches of The Spectrum, including wheelchair-bound non-verbal kids and kids so dysfunctional that I could not imagine what their lives held for them. Many of the parents appeared to be so drained and exhausted, hollow-looking, and I wondered what their day was like, and if some of them might be so tired that they merely dropped off their kids and went home to sleep. As for me, I ran errands in town, visited farmer friends out east of Pueblo, and shopped for groceries before returning to pick up Harrison for the day. I usually felt exhausted as well.

One day upon arriving in the morning I noticed a child face down in fenced-in playground. He seemed to be just floundering in the dirt. When I took Harrison inside I notified the staff about this child. They didn't seem too excited. In the mornings Pueblo West didn't seem too bad, but most afternoons when I returned to Soaring Eagles to pick up Harrison were quite different. The summer heat had begun to work on the nearby waste-collection center, rendering a stench that I could hardly bear. I kept the windows rolled up out of concern the rotten odor would infiltrate my groceries, and also because there was often a hot breeze raising dust and spinning whirlwinds along with it. And then I'd go inside and watch the sad parade of parents returning to get their kids, most of whom appeared much more severely affected than Harrison, though many of them also seemed easier for their parents to manage. It was sometimes a struggle for me to get Harrison to the car as he sometimes would fixate on the doors on the way out and refuse to leave. Often as we drove away from that place, with the dust and tumbleweeds flying by in the blast-furnace breeze and dust-devils, I felt as if I were in Hell. I could see the mountains through the haze and think of where I would much rather be, and of things I'd much rather be doing. But for now I just had to accept where I was.

Once I had to wait for quite some time for Harrison. There had been some sort of issue with his behavior at the day's end and they were working through it with him. All the other parents had since retrieved their kids, and I could hear an occasional outburst in the back. I also could overhear conversations in the staff room and one of the workers was describing how one of the kids had been striking out, hitting. The way she was talking about it, this seemed like an everyday occurrence for these employees. I tuned in to this because in recent weeks Harrison had begun to strike out more often as well. It wasn't like he hadn't done this from time to time previously, but it seemed to have been much worse recently. Now I wondered if he'd seen other kids do this at Soaring Eagles and perhaps was imitating the behavior, much the same way he'd imitated noises from his previous experience there.

Curtis called one evening and we were talking about my training with Boogie and I told him I'd been spending way too much time at the wheel lately, driving

Harrison to Soaring Eagles. "What is that, a summer camp?" he asked.

I thought about that for a moment and then answered, "No . . . it's really more like an institution."

It was then that I knew we had to decrease our involvement with the program. It was too stressful commuting to and from the center, and it was not what I wanted for Harrison. I talked it over with the director and we cut back on the weekly sessions until the program ended.

One day when we left Soaring Eagles Harrison somehow had the idea that we were going into Pueblo. When I made the right turn toward the mountains and home he screamed, unbuckled his seat belt, then leaped forward and struck me while I was driving. Startled by having this happen while in traffic, I yelled loudly at him to stop and to sit back down. He did so but was still protesting loudly, and now he was upset with my reaction. I pulled into a convenience store for fuel.

I sat there behind the wheel and took a deep breath. And then I tried to talk to him. I told him we were going home, and that what he did was very dangerous, and that we could have gotten into an accident, hurt, or killed. I told him I was sorry that I yelled at him like that but that he had startled me, and that he could not do that while I was driving. He quieted down as I got out to pump the gasoline. He seemed to be thinking it over. When I got back inside, he said, "You know what?"

"What?"

"When we get home I'm going to make you an 'I'm sorry' card."

"OK. That's a deal."

~

The wildfire season in Colorado and The West in general was intense, and the smoke from the fires hindered my training efforts. One major blaze about 100 miles to the West often filled our air with smoke, depending on the prevailing wind. I would watch the plume trailing from the blaze as it shifted north to south, and try to time my workouts accordingly as running in the smoke seemed counterproductive. On one occasion I waited all day before heading out with Boogie in the clean evening air, only to have an umber shadow appear about three miles out and then be enveloped in heavy smoke before we arrived back home from the workout. The prevailing wind had shifted just slightly. One evening the smoke was so thick at our house that we seriously feared for our health. Ultimately Mary and I packed up camping gear and Harrison, and drove south to San Isabel, where her brother owns a cabin, in order to sleep. We arrived back the next morning to clear blue skies but later the smoke moved back in.

The last weeks leading up to the World Championship were upon me and I knew I wanted to get Boogie and myself above timberline at least once. The timing was tricky given the smoke pollution and the threat of thunderstorms. Plus, I didn't have the spare time or want to spend gas money driving to Fairplay to run Mosquito Pass. So I started eyeing a nearby mountain pass where I'd trained for the race many years ago.

Hermit Pass rises to over 13,000 feet, about 5,000 feet above the Wet Mountain Valley floor. From the valley it was possible to get in a climb bigger than the Fairplay course with much of it above timberline. The problem was that I was having trouble motivating to spend a day doing this alone, and also timing this workout around the weather conditions and life in general. My friend Tracy was also looking for a long workout. She'd taken up pack-burro racing just a couple of years prior and I'd been loaning her burros for the races. The previous summer she'd kept and trained Spike in Boulder and had been the first female finisher, and third place overall, in the World Championship. She was not able to run the Fairplay race this summer because of a social commitment, but was hoping to get in a run with Laredo, who I'd loaned to her, as training for the remaining two races of the season at Leadville and Buena Vista. So we made tentative plans to run Hermit Pass, allowing that if the weather looked bad or the smoke too thick we'd bail.

Miraculously, the day arrived crisp and blue, like it had been transported from late September or early October. We parked the truck and trailer at the western edge of the valley that morning and started up the pass with Laredo and Boogie. As we climbed the lower part of the pass the ponderosa pines and oak brush gave way to aspen and spruce-fir forests. The road seemed rockier and rougher than I remembered and the going was slow. The bright sun was bringing out a sweat on the burros and at one point a swarm of horse flies descended on the animals. I found some arnica flowers near the road and rubbed them on the burros' noses and the flies disappeared.

Up, up, up. We continued on and talked about our lives in general. She was 35 and engaged to be married in the fall. Her previous boyfriend had committed suicide and she still harbored pain and guilt from that experience. She loathed her career as a packaging engineer, and longed to do something more creative, maybe write. The biological clock was ticking but she wasn't sure she wanted to have children. Despite her high income, she admitted she was not good at saving money and was spending her savings on a wedding dress and a month-long honeymoon trip.

I listened to Tracy as we climbed the pass, and thought back upon my own life choices, the trail that had led me to where I was today. I'd learned so many things over the course of my life but in the final analysis this pool of knowledge had amounted to very little in the big scheme of the Universe. Every choice I'd made — good or bad, large or small, right or wrong — had led me precisely to that place where, for whatever reason, I needed to be. As George Harrison had borrowed from

Lewis Carroll's *Alice in Wonderland* for his song "Any Road": "If you don't know where you're going, any road'll take you there." The truthful irony is nobody really knows where they are going — the idea that anyone is in control of their own destiny is really just an illusion.

For now the only road that mattered was the one beneath our feet. This road we traveled on this day took us through the highest stands of dwarf aspens and stunted spruce trees, and finally led us out above the timberline to sweeping views of tundra and rock as far as the eyes could see. Wildflowers studded the landscape, turquoise lakes spread out below us and an azure sky lighted our way. Pikas and marmots, small mammals that inhabit these high places, let out their shrill calls that echoed off the rocks. Otherwise all was quiet. And still the road through the talus climbed onward, through a series of switchbacks, along a narrow ridge, arriving at last at the final pitch to the summit. Here crystal-clear snowmelt ran off the sidewalls and onto the road. Snowbanks glistened in the sunshine, and one covered the road and part of a little trail that skirted off to the side.

I jumped up onto the bank and tugged on Boogie to climb up off the road. Tracy urged her on from behind, and then Tracy tried to lead Laredo up and he refused. At last I decided to leave Boogie and jump down to haze Laredo up off the roadbed. In doing so I slipped on the snowbank, my feet shot out from underneath me and I flew a short distance on the steep slope, landing on the packed snow with a painfully hard splash and then sliding on my ass until regaining my footing on the road. I was slightly embarrassed and jumped up immediately to get Laredo moving. It was slow picking our way through the rocks, loose dirt and tufts of grass around the snowbank, and so steep that all we could see was the slope and blue sky above. But I knew the top was just right there so we continued. At one point Tracy yelled upwards, "Is this safe?"

I yelled back down. "No, it isn't safe. Life isn't safe, Tracy!" And in a very few minutes we were standing on the Hermit Pass summit, 13,078 feet above sea level, where a giant fat marmot lay sunning on a big dark rock, the peaks of the Sangre de Cristos were lined up north-to-south like the gates to heaven and the entire world spread out below us. My mind shot back to that first time I'd summited Mosquito Pass with Moose so long ago, and it shot forward to the race just a few weeks ahead. If nothing else, the quest at least had led me to this place, here and now. And now was good enough.

తా

It rained most of the night before the race, and when my alarm went off I seriously considered going right back to bed. My mind rushed back to that gray day in April when Boogie had behaved so oddly in the fog. As I drove to Fairplay that morning the clouds were hanging tight to the mountains and Mosquito Pass was completely shrouded in black. I wondered what I was doing there, and as I prepared for the start in the sprinkling rain I felt totally discombobulated. Even my socks seemed to not be fitting right. Once while reaching into my pickup for something I slipped on the wet running board and banged my shin. I felt vaguely like the Clint Eastwood character in the movie *Unforgiven,* unable to get in the saddle. I almost forgot to put Boogie's hoof boots on and remembered them only a few minutes before the start. I had arranged for my friend Carol Marra and her partner Lee Hall to crew for me and as they watched my chaotic preparation for the race I could see the looks of doubt on their faces. Carol had crewed for me the year I'd won my first championship and I couldn't help but think she must have been thinking how much I'd aged since then. When I arrived at the starting line I didn't have my race number. A race official noticed this and issued another one to me. Then the gun fired and we were off.

Boogie seemed focused on the task at hand. We gradually worked our way to near the front of the pack of 52 teams and then just watched. George and his burro Jack were already vying for the lead in the first few miles, and meanwhile I was dealing with a sock problem. Pack-burro racing is a lot like life — it's not a matter of whether something will go wrong. It's how you handle what goes wrong. My right sock had slipped down the ankle and was bunched underneath the arch of my foot. For some reason during that chaotic preparation before the race I had put a spare mismatched sock in my saddle bags. I found an opportune moment to grab it and put it in my shorts pocket. A couple miles later at a water stop I pulled Boogie up and managed to remove the one sock and quickly put my shoe back on, losing several places in the process. We caught back up to the lead pack over the course of the next couple miles.

At the next checkpoint I stopped and quickly put the fresh sock on the sockless foot. An old blister on my achilles had opened up and was bleeding. Four teams were now jockeying for the lead, but soon George and I were able to pull away as the climb grew steeper. We reached the base of London Mountain near timberline in good time and I thought how we were only about one-third of the way and all the most difficult terrain lay ahead. Next, a steep climb up the South London hill where Boogie and I got a short-lived lead on George before reaching American Flats. After crossing the first stream I felt the left sock begin to slip, and by the time we were on the tundra the burros were not moving very well and we could see Karen Thorpe and Kokomo catching up to us very quickly. Karen soon caught and passed us, then led the way through the narrow passage through the steep boulder field that would put us out on the Mosquito Pass just a short distance below the summit. She reached the top first, followed closely by George and myself. There the wind was howling out of the gray sky. After circling the marker at the top I stopped and removed the other failing sock and knew I'd have to run the 15 miles back to town without a sock on that foot. George's burro Jack wouldn't go ahead and Boogie was stalled out, too. By the time he and I got the animals moving again Karen was almost out of sight on the descent.

Over the course of the next couple miles we gradually caught back up to Karen, then she stopped to adjust her saddle and George and I went ahead. We were now in the realm beyond 20 miles and what ensued was another race within the race. I pushed back the memories of the year before when I had taken a hard fall and George had just gradually pulled away and won. As the pace quickened I felt like the earth was flowing beneath me and I prayed I would not trip or stumble as I'd done the previous year. There were times I felt as though I was running on the edge of my capabilities. Several times George and Jack pulled ahead and even vanished around curves But then Jack would stall out by turning off into a ditch or simply stopping, and each time Boogie was right there. I had the fleeting thought that we had them right where we wanted them but then there was the reality that we still had eight miles to go and anything could happen. Boogie held to her big smooth trot towing me psychically along. Whenever George would pull away I would dig deep within and run on. I kept telling myself that I could not let up, could not let him go. Not this time.

Which is how we found ourselves in the final few miles trading places over and over again, with neither burro willing to leave the other. At one point George pulled ahead and Jack simply put on the brakes. Boogie stopped. George turned to me and opened his arms. We embraced as friends then continued on as competitors. When at last we came to the narrow trail that leads up to Fairplay and the finish line, George and Jack were ahead. They topped the final hill ahead of us and we started down into town. Boogie drew up alongside Jack and then Jack pulled ahead again. The burros trotted down the street weaving slightly and picking up speed as we approached the finish line. Faster and faster.

Then just a few feet out, Jack cracked under the pressure and veered left, almost into the crowd. As George scrambled to collect Jack, Boogie seized the moment. I saw her ears go forward and she bolted for the finish — her feet hardly touching the ground. I knew even before she got there that we had won and as time stood still one more time for me I held up my hands as her nose crossed the finish line, five fingers on one and two on the other — seven wins.

As the crowd cheered and people mobbed me, Carol reached over the top of the throng and handed me a cell phone. "Did you win?" said the voice on the other end. I was having troubling hearing and gathering my words, and then realized it was Mary. "Did you win?" she repeated.

"Yeah, we won! We passed them right near the finish . . . I still can't believe it."

The crowd was still loud and it was difficult to hear. Then I heard a commotion followed by Harrison screaming on the other end. "Oh, I better go," she said. "I love you."

"I love you too."

I handed the phone back to Carol and then took in the hugs, handshakes and congratulations of longtime friends and complete strangers. Boogie and I had accomplished the improbable. In this moment I felt the tears of gratitude and joy on my cheeks. For all that has been and all that was to follow.

∾

A few weeks later as I was pulling away from the feed store in Westcliffe one evening I noticed the low sunlight on the headstones of the small cemetery on the hillside about a mile away. I've seen so many great photos of cemeteries in the Southwest, and had tried some photography in this graveyard a couple of times with no luck. But this evening the light and the clouds looked interesting and I thought I'd drive up there and take a look around.

Harrison and I got out of the car and stepped across the cattle guard and into the fenced-in cemetery. There was a warm breeze and the little flags on the veterans' graves all fluttered in unison. It seems there's always a breeze at this cemetery. But it's one of the most peaceful places I know. Harrison began running around looking at the headstones, reading the names, some of them of well-known Wet Mountain Valley families.

For the past few years it's been common for us to hang out at the playground after school lets out so Harrison can play with the other kids. But he had become less interested in the playground or his friends, and more commonly bothered other parents, asking for their cell phones or their keys, and interrupting conversations. One afternoon his behavior escalated to a point that I realized I needed to physically remove him from the playground. Like so many of these incidents over the years, after it's over it's all a blur, difficult to remember the sequence of events and the deciding factor that led to the decision to take extreme measures. He had been rude to his friends and their parents. He had yelled and screamed. He had talked back when I asked him to stop, and continued on with the misbehavior. At some point I took his backpack over to the car then returned to pick him up and carry him kicking and screaming and swinging from the playground with a group of parents of neurotypical children as an audience. I know deep inside few of these people could do what I just did without the guidance of both a personal trainer and a psychotherapist. This is the sort of behavior and consequences one might expect when dealing with much younger children, but at 9 years old it's physically like picking up and carrying a very uncooperative and loud bale of hay, and psychologically as flattening as being run over by a truck. Afterward strikes the realization that as a parent I could avoid this entire scene repeating itself by simply avoiding the playground altogether.

Now Harrison was running around the graveyard like it was a playground. He asked if it was a maze. I told him no, that this was a cemetery, and anticipated the next question but there was none. In recent months he'd had questions about both birth and death. I'd tried to explain as best as I could, keeping in mind that such abstract notions seem the most difficult for the autistic mind to reason. How does one relate the veritable shortness and unpredictability of life to someone whose concrete way of understanding the world around them so radically and profoundly alters the way they perceive life itself? I recalled the sheer terror when I was about his age and learned about death and that some people were buried after they died. I stayed awake at night in a claustrophobic panic at this notion. I didn't want Harrison to have this same experience, but then many grown-ups battle with this fear.

We walked the little two-track dirt road through the graveyard, and I focused on a tall white cross with some headstones and iron grave fences behind it, puffy clouds for a backdrop. I took several shots at different angles. I knew the images were somewhat less awesome than, say, Ansel Adams' *Moonrise, Hernandez, New Mexico* for example.

When I turned around I found Harrison sitting in a painted white wrought-iron bench at the foot of a nearby grave. As I walked up to him I could see the massive and dark-polished stone, the actual grave covered in decorative gravel — white with a red pattern. Harrison was inspecting a weathered teddy bear that was wired to the bench to keep the ever-present wind from carrying it away. I looked to the stone and saw the grave belonged to a girl who had died when she was 15.

"What is this?" Harrison asked.

"Well . . . it's the grave of a girl who died," I said. "She's buried here."

"Let's dig her out," he said with an air of concern.

"No, son, she's gone . . . her spirit lives on but her body is dead. Just her body is buried here."

"Is her spirit gone to outer space?"

"No, her spirit is in heaven. This is a just a place where her family can come and sit and remember her, and talk to her."

"OK."

We walked down the little two-track road and I paused to take more pictures. Harrison read more names from the stones. I surveyed the little cemetery and its collection of graves. A big white stone Santo stood at the entrance with arms outstretched. The graves were marked with everything from simple hand-painted wooden crosses and small flagstone slabs to ornate granite and marble stones, some with spires and crosses.

Fences surrounded some of the plots. Little pots of plastic flowers adorned others.

We walked back to the car. I looked through the windshield at the sweeping range of the valley, the jagged Sangre de Cristo mountains towering above. Because of my childhood fear of being buried I'd always wanted to be cremated, but I thought if I were to change my mind this would be the place to be. On the wind there was the sound of music, like someone playing a flute very badly. I stuck my head out the window trying to determine what this sound was and where it was coming from. I asked Harrison if he heard it too and he said he did.

Finally I stood back out of the car and listened. The sound was coming from the cemetery. Perhaps some wind flute over a grave, or the breeze breathing through a fence, a headstone or some other ornament placed by those left behind. Or perhaps the music of a friendly spirit playing a tune to a weathered teddy bear.

~

With burros they're either alive or they're dead. It happens that suddenly. Harrison was home on the day when Clyde crossed over, and was very much a witness to much of the very short process. With the help of neighbors we were able to move the carcass onto a small flatbed trailer and pull it with a four-wheeler over to a small aspen grove on our property where we gave Clyde back to the earth.

At 30, Clyde was not all that old for a burro. But he'd lived a very full and adventuresome life. I first saw Clyde a day after he was born in 1983. He was a small burro but had a spirit larger than any animal I've ever known. I won my first pack-burro race in Chama, New Mexico, with him in 1985, and later he won the Leadville Boom Days race. We'd also had many adventures packing in the backcountry. Over the years he had saved my lunch and broke my heart in races. Though he never won a World Championship he placed second many times and elevated me to that place where I could find the confidence to win it with Spike and other burros. His passing marked another end to an animal's era.

With Clyde's death Harrison seemed more engaged in the sense of loss than he had been with Ted. Later we went for a walk and he asked, "Do you know where Clyde is?"

"He's in heaven," I said.

"Where is heaven?"

"It's all around us."

"Are we in heaven?"

"Yes."

⁊

It was a beautiful October day and the weather report said snow and freezing temperatures were on the way. I called my farmer friend Doug to ask about the peppers and he said "you better get out here." I decided to take Harrison out of school early and try to squeeze in a couple of hours of pepper-picking. We drove out to Avondale, stopping at a food stand for water and a cookie on our way.

Harrison was thrilled to get out of school early. And for the first time he seemed interested in picking vegetables, and intrigued with the idea of saving them for the winter. We walked through the rows with shopping bags, then returned to our starting point to empty them into boxes. We had two big farm boxes and the peppers we had picked nearly filled both of them. I figured one more shopping bag would top off both boxes. We were there, after all, and there were still lots of peppers in the field. They would be gone with the frost tomorrow. I could see José in the distance at the far end of the pepper patch picking madly through the rows.

As we worked our way back to the car, our bag nearly full, it was irresistible to pass by any pepper that appeared ripe and still firm. The bag was nearly full as I paused and kneeled to inspect a red pepper on a vine.

"Hey, do you want me here?" said a little voice right at my level as I kneeled by the pepper plant.

"Well, of course I want you here. That's why I took you out of school early and we drove all the way out here."

He looked down at the ground, searching for his words. The October sun felt warm as he considered the double meaning of what he'd said and then stumbled with his own language to ask me in his own words if I was glad that he'd been born.

Time stood still for a moment there in a field of peppers washed by the golden sun with the mountains as a distant backdrop. I thought of all the struggles, frustrations, stresses and challenges that Harrison's presence had presented over the last nine years. How there is only the way forward. The acceptance of what is. The truth.

"Yes, son, I am."

First Christmas, 2004. (Photo by Patrick O'Grady)

Mary, Harrison, Spike, and Redbo, on the Music Pass Summit, 2007.

Harrison as the No. 2, Halloween in
Westcliffe, 2012.

Harrison and Laredo at Dry Lake high in the Sangre
de Cristo Range.

Mary and Harrison waiting in line at the Kit Carson Home in Taos, New Mexico, to get into the park for the Mumford and Sons concert.

Heading out on the World Championship course.
(Photo by Amber Canterbury)

Full Tilt Boogie and Hal winning the 28.6-mile World Championship in Fairplay, 2013. (Photo by Bonnie Wann)

Picking peppers at Larga Vista Ranch.

Made in the USA
Columbia, SC
31 August 2017